INSTRUCTOR'S MANUAL

SPEAKING SOLUTIONS

INTERACTION, PRESENTATION, LISTENING, AND PRONUNCIATION SKILLS

Candace Matthews

The George Washington University

Acquisitions Editor: *Nancy Baxer*
Director of Production and Manufacturing: *David Riccardi*
Electronic Production Coordinator: *Molly Pike Riccardi*

Editorial Production / Design Manager: *Dominick Mosco*
Electronic/production supervision: *Paula D. Williams*
Cover Design Coordinator: *Merle Krumper/Paul Belfanti*
Production Coordinator: *Ray Keating*

Printed in the United States of America

17 18 19 20   OPM   10 09 08

ISBN 0-13-100603-7

CONTENTS

I. INTRODUCTION

A. Purpose of the Course

The purpose of *Speaking Solutions: Interaction, Presentation, Listening, and Pronunciation Skills* is to develop the oral communication skills of intermediate through advanced ESL/EFL students in academic and professional settings. The text is intended for use in pre-academic college classes, intensive ESL/EFL programs, private language schools, and English training courses for professionals. The text has been designed with an international market in mind, so it is appropriate for both international students in English speaking countries as well as students in non-English speaking countries.

B. Course Planning

The best way to start planning the course is to read the Preface, the Contents, and Appendix A in the text. The Preface provides an overview of the text and includes a number of suggestions for using the material. The Contents shows how the book is organized and Appendix A includes evaluation forms which explain the evaluation criteria.

C. Time Schedule

The text is designed for one semester of instruction. With an abundance of material, the text can be used selectively to meet the needs of your students and to fit the time available. Clearly, the approach you use in covering different sections of the text can greatly affect the amount of time you spend on each unit. If time is limited, you may move through the material more quickly by trying some of the following:

- Omit any sections or activities that are not directly relevant to the needs of your class. For example, you might consider some of the activities in the sections on Cross-Cultural Communication or Learning Strategies as optional.

- Assign students to read appropriate sections of the text as homework and then review the important ideas briefly in class. This frees up class time for activities.

- In activities that include several different situations, limit the number of situations that students discuss.

1

- Have students do all individual work (such as filling in charts) as homework, not in class.

- Have students give some of their presentations simultaneously to small groups of students rather than one-by-one to the entire class.

- Have students do some (if not all) of the listening and pronunciation activities in a language laboratory. If a language lab is not available, try to arrange for your students to have access to the tape and a tape recorder outside of class.

D. Overview of the Text

The Preface of the text includes a brief overview of how the text is organized. Unit 0 is designed to help students get acquainted with one another and to provide you with some basic information about each student. These introductory activities are important in creating a positive, relaxed class atmosphere in which the students feel comfortable expressing their ideas.

Units 1 through 7 follow the same format. Each unit is introduced by a warm-up page of photographs and discussion questions that are designed to stimulate an informal exchange of ideas in the classroom. Students can work in pairs or in small groups to discuss the answers to the questions and then share ideas as a class. Of course, you may wish to develop other questions or activities to exploit these photographs further.

Each unit is divided into sections:

Listening Practice: It is extremely important for you to review these activities in advance in order to decide whether to use each activity to **introduce** a particular skill or to **reinforce** the skill after covering it in the Communication Skills section. The instructions may advise reviewing a particular section before covering the activity. In this case, you may want to postpone the listening activity until after you have covered the appropriate section in the text.

If you do the Listening Practice activities in class, be sure to go over the explanation and instructions for each activity before playing the tape. In this way, you can make sure that students understand the task or tasks that they are going to do. Then, as students listen or after they have listened to that activity on the tape, they can complete the task. In some activities, it may be necessary for you to pause the tape to allow enough time for students to write their answers. When there are different tasks for an activity, you can rewind the tape and play that section again.

In many cases, students may need to listen to each activity several times in order to focus on both content and language use. To maximize active student interaction in class, you might have students do many of these listening activities outside of class, if possible. One common approach is to introduce and begin a listening activity in class and then assign students to finish it as homework. In this way, students with poor listening skills can listen to the tape as many times as they need to in order to complete the activity. You can then briefly review the answers to each activity in class.

Communication Skills: Most of the "hard" information is presented in this section. As mentioned in the Preface of the text, it is not an efficient use of class time to read this material aloud. One way to deal with the information is to assign parts of it as homework, and then use class time to review and discuss the important points briefly. Another possibility is to assign individual students to take charge of presenting certain parts of the text. You can find more specific information on group activities and presentations in other sections in this manual.

Pronunciation Practice: As with the Listening Practice section, you may assign students to do these activities outside of class. This allows students with pronunciation problems to repeat the pronunciation activities as often as necessary. If some students in your class have especially serious pronunciation problems, you might want to use a supplementary or optional text to provide additional pronunciation practice. An excellent text (with four accompanying audiotapes) for this purpose is *Sound Advantage: A Pronunciation Book* by Stacy A. Hagen and Patricia E. Grogan (Englewood Cliffs, New Jersey: Regents/Prentice Hall, 1992).

Learning Strategies: The activities in this section help the students learn how to analyze their language learning strategies. Thus, students are able to take more responsibility for their own learning.

Cross-Cultural Communication: The activities in this section provide students with a brief exposure to some cross cultural issues that may be of interest to them. Where appropriate, an Answer Key provides answers from a "typical" American point of view.

3

E. Pace

In a course such as this, it is extremely important to keep the class moving at a relatively fast pace that maintains high student interest. To do this, you may need to set time limits for each activity. Generally, students work more efficiently if they know they have to achieve a certain objective within a limited amount of time. You can find further information about setting time limits in the sections on Group Activities and Oral Presentations in this manual.

F. Variety of Activities

This text includes more activities than you will probably have time to cover in your course. Occasionally, however, you may want to add your own personal touches to the course. Students will find class more enjoyable if it is sometimes unpredictable. Bring in music or ask students to bring in some of their favorite songs in English. Have students fill in a cloze passage as they listen to a popular song. Teach the class a folk song. Bring in a guest speaker to give a brief talk. Watch a video. Bring in a cartoon or comic strip from the newspaper to discuss. Play a word game. Bring in a current newspaper article for students to discuss.

G. Correspondence

If you have any questions, comments, or suggestions, please feel free to contact me:

Candace Matthews
The George Washington University
EFL Program, Academic Center T-604
801 22nd Street N.W.
Washington, D.C. 20052

Office telephone: (202) 994-7136

E-mail address:
Bitnet: matt@gwuvm
Internet: matt@gwuvm.gwu.edu

II.   THE ROLE OF THE TEACHER

A. Establishing a Supportive Class Atmosphere

Because the social climate in the classroom has such a strong impact on learning, it is extremely important for you to create a relaxed, supportive class atmosphere. In such an atmosphere, students feel free to ask questions and express their ideas without being overly worried about making mistakes. This requires an accepting and encouraging attitude on your part. A good sense of humor also helps. While it is never appropriate to make fun of students or laugh at their mistakes, you can certainly appreciate the natural humor that arises spontaneously in class. A reasonable amount of humor and laughter in class generally has a positive, relaxing effect on the class atmosphere. The point is to encourage students not to take themselves or their mistakes too seriously.

Mutual respect is an important element of building a class atmosphere that is conducive to learning. Students generally respond positively to a teacher who shows a sincere interest in them as individuals. For this reason, it is important to learn your students' names as soon as possible and use them freely. It may help to spend a few minutes at the beginning of each class period chatting informally with your students. Find out what some of them did the night before, what they did last weekend, etc. Get them to ask each other these types of questions. Of course, it is important not to use up too much class time with this type of questioning, but a brief period of informal chatting at the beginning of class can help maintain a friendly class atmosphere.

You may find that students coming from more traditional language learning backgrounds feel uncomfortable and insecure in a learner-centered classroom. These students may feel skeptical (at best!) about the value of pair and group work since they are accustomed to relying on the teacher as the source of knowledge and the arbiter of correctness. If you feel that a number of your students have negative attitudes toward pair and group work, you might find it helpful to bring this issue out in the open. Encourage students to discuss their expectations of the roles that teachers and students "should" play in the classroom. Discuss/elicit the advantages that pair and group work offer a class. In fact, Activity 3 in the Listening Practice section of Unit 3 focuses on some of the advantages of group work. However, you may want to discuss this issue earlier in the course.

5

B. Managing the Class

While a learner-centered class involves a high degree of student responsibility and involvement, the teacher still has full responsibility for carefully structuring the class. In general, here are some guidelines (in no particular order) for conducting class:

- Plan lessons with varied activities that balance individual, pair, group, and class work.

- Keep teacher talk to a bare minimum. Keep students involved at all times by eliciting as much information as possible rather than providing it yourself.

- Encourage students to listen to each other in class discussions by not repeating what they say; let students take responsibility for asking one another to repeat or clarify something.

- Encourage self- and peer-correction before offering teacher correction (when correction is appropriate).

- Ensure that all students have equal opportunity to participate in class discussions.

- Encourage students to consider their own progress without making comparisons to others in the class.

- Be sensitive to cultural differences. If students seem uncomfortable discussing a particular topic, skip that topic, substitute a different one, or develop one of your own.

- Make your system of evaluation or grading clear to students from the beginning of the course.

- Counsel uncooperative, disruptive, talkative, or withdrawn students individually, outside of class; do not let one or two students with attitude problems affect the class atmosphere.

C. Presenting the Material

In a learner-centered course such as this, your primary goal is to promote student involvement and interaction. Therefore, you do not want to take up class time by lecturing or reading the material aloud. As much as possible, cover the material by assigning a section or sections as homework, reviewing the information briefly, and then devoting class time to activities.

Setting up an activity involves: (1) providing clear, concise instructions; (2) making sure that students know exactly what is expected of them at the end of the activity, such as written answers in their texts, a group report, etc.; (3) setting appropriate time limits; and (4) providing feedback or some type of follow-up upon completion of the activity. If an activity involves observation or evaluation, students should look over the appropriate form before beginning the activity. You may also want to prepare students for some activities by presenting, eliciting, or reviewing vocabulary, structures, discussion skills, etc. that they may need in completing a particular activity. You can then encourage students to practice these points as they work through the activity.

Each unit includes a number of shaded boxes that highlight useful expressions for conveying a variety of language functions. The expressions listed in each box are limited to some examples, neutral/polite in style, that are generally appropriate in academic and professional settings. These lists of expressions are intended to be used as a reference source. You and the students may want to add further expressions to these lists as you work through the unit. You can also encourage students to use these expressions as they participate in the activities. Before going over the lists provided, you can discuss each function and then have students work individually or in small groups to list expressions they are already familiar with. As a class, you might discuss possible situations in which these expressions could appropriately be used.

D. Selecting Appropriate Activities

It is important to spend time selecting the activities that are the most relevant to your students' interests and needs. Within each activity, you may want to select one or two situations for discussion when more are offered. You should definitely not feel that you need to cover every section, every activity, or every situation within an activity. For instance, with advanced students, you may work quickly through the first two units of the text, covering a limited number of activities, in order to spend more time on the later units. With intermediate level students, you can work more slowly through the units, omitting Unit 7 if time is a problem.

E. Monitoring Activities

In general, your purpose is to monitor group activities, not to take part in them. Students gain a sense of achievement by learning how to sustain an activity on their own. If you participate in a group activity, students may be tempted to rely on you to keep the activity going, to solve communication problems, or to provide "correct" answers. At the same time, you may find it difficult to give students the necessary freedom to make their own mistakes if you are a group participant.

When students are working on activities, you should circulate from group to group. This allows you to discover problems students may be having and helps ensure that students are on task and are using English. While you do not want to intrude on pair or group work, you should stay involved in what the students are doing. Some students may begin (or continue) to doubt the usefulness of pair and group work if you withdraw by sitting at your desk or by leaving the room. The idea is to build an invisible glass wall between you and the students, so they are aware of your presence, but do not try to involve you in the task. The best way to keep from being drawn into group interaction is by avoiding eye contact with group members. Depending on the seating arrangement, you may want to pull up a chair or sit in a desk slightly behind the group.

As you circulate, you can keep track of the kinds of problems students are having — grammatical accuracy, word choice, pronunciation/intonation, discussion strategies, etc. The most important problems, of course, are those that interfere with communication. The best way to deal with these problems is to make mental notes of what you observe and occasionally "wander" back to your desk to make written notes. Students may become inhibited if they feel you are making a list of all their mistakes. You may use the information you collect while circulating as the basis for post-activity feedback or for future lessons.

Students should get in the habit of dealing with any problems they have without your assistance. You should encourage group members to rely on one another to supply unknown vocabulary words, clarify unclear comments or questions, deal with communication breakdowns, etc. Then, if group members cannot resolve the problem, they can turn to you for necessary

8

assistance. You may also find it necessary to intervene if a group has gone off task or is facing other serious problems.

You may want to take part (very) occasionally in group discussions with a particular purpose in mind. For example, you might play the role of "devil's advocate" to challenge students to defend their points of view. This role is especially useful if all the group members reach agreement without considering different sides of an issue. Another reason to join a group **briefly** is to give group members practice in dealing with a difficult situation. In this case, you may participate by taking a negative role in the discussion by interrupting excessively, changing the topic inappropriately, adding irrelevant comments, or speaking aggressively. Of course, students should know in advance that you will be taking on a negative role on purpose; otherwise, they will not respond appropriately. This kind of "play acting" should not be carried on so long that it stops participants from working productively. However, it is often easier for students to practice dealing with troublesome behavior from the teacher (knowing that it is intentional, to give them practice) rather than trying to deal with a peer in a more realistic situation.

F. Correcting Mistakes

This course involves a gradual build-up of the students' oral communication skills. While working to develop these skills, students should expect to make mistakes. In fact, these mistakes are quite useful since students will be learning to analyze them in order to improve their skills.

One important concern in correcting students is your attitude. You do not want to be seen as the authority figure in the classroom, listening to students just so you can correct every mistake they make. You are there to monitor the students' performance, but that does not mean you should correct all of their mistakes. When you decide it is appropriate to deal with problems, your approach should be, "Okay, what do think went wrong? Why did it happen? How can you correct it? What can you do so it doesn't happen again?" This type of approach will help students develop their own strategies to overcome their problems.

Another issue you may face is deciding what kind of mistakes to correct. It is important not to try to correct every mistake that students make during a discussion or presentation. In general, you want to focus on mistakes that interfere with communication or interaction.

9

You also need to decide when to correct the students. The general rule is not to correct students' mistakes while an activity is going on. When students are interacting, they should be focusing on communicating their ideas, not worrying about possible mistakes. An effective way of dealing with most problems is to keep a record of the mistakes you notice as you are listening to discussions and presentations. With pair or group work, you can point out a few of the most serious errors, especially ones that noticeably interfered with communication, at the end of an activity. You may repeat the incorrect sentence or write it on the board and have students try to correct the mistake. With individual presentations, you can note serious mistakes on the evaluation form to draw students' attention to their errors. In other cases, you may decide not to mention specific errors, but you can plan future language lessons to deal with the problems you identified.

G. Using Videotape

Excellent use can be made of videotape in a course such as this. If videotaping facilities are available, make a tape of group discussions or individual presentations. You can then show these tapes to the individuals involved, to small groups, or to the entire class for analysis and/or evaluation. With presentations, you might schedule individual appointments outside of class to meet with students on a one-to-one basis to discuss the strengths and weaknesses of the presentation. While this is an excellent opportunity to provide individual attention to students, it may require more time than you have available. Another way to deal with presentations is to provide students with written evaluations and then make the tape of student presentations available so each student can review his or her performance individually.

With small group work, you can stop the tape to focus on appropriate or inappropriate interaction. While observing a group discussion, you can ask such questions as:

"What happened here?"
"What did the speaker just say?"
"How does this relate to what the previous speaker said?"
"What could or should the speaker have said here?"
"Should the leader or another group member have said something here?"

Of course, you should also stop the tape to point out particularly relevant or useful kinds of comments. Since this kind of analysis requires close attention, you might review short segments instead of an entire discussion. Students benefit from this activity only as long as they are paying careful attention, so be sensitive to the length of their attention span.

You may find it useful to save a videotape from your current class to use with future classes. Students often benefit from seeing an example of a good discussion group or an effective presentation early in the course to understand clearly what their goals are. Keep in mind, though, that some students may have very strong (negative) feelings about your showing a video in which they are speaking. For this reason, you should consider obtaining permission from students before using videotapes in which they appear.

III. GROUP ACTIVITIES

A. Determining Group Size

Groups composed of four students seem to work out the best. With this number, students feel a sense of responsibility for the outcome of their group work. Three or five students per group is all right. With six or more students in a group, the sense of individual responsibility seems to grow weaker — students feel more anonymous, lost in the crowd. Interaction is reduced since individuals have less chance to participate. Also, in a larger group there is a greater likelihood that weak or quiet students will be left out of the discussion. With three or fewer students per group, excessive demands are put on individual participants.

B. Setting up Activities

Most of the activities in the text are self-explanatory. When working in small groups, students should take on the roles of leader, reader, summarizer, etc. as explained and practiced in "Organizing Small Group Activities" in the Communication Skills section of Unit 1. In this way, students take full responsibility for completing the activity. Furthermore, students gain regular practice in leading discussions, summarizing, reporting results, and so forth. If you feel that you need to give instructions, be sure to do so <u>before</u> students move into groups. Before beginning an activity, students should know exactly what their task is and approximately how long they have to accomplish it.

C. Arranging Seating

The seating arrangement in the classroom should be very flexible. Students can group their desks into tight circles when working in groups. If they are sitting at tables, students can group around a table — two on one side, two on the other. In any case, group members should always sit so that they can easily maintain eye contact with each other.

D. Selecting Groups

It usually works best to keep recombining students into different groups to work on different activities. This helps students learn to adjust to people with different personalities and different language abilities. With set groups, students may get used to a certain pattern of interaction, with the same people tending to take leadership roles. You may let students choose their groups or assign them to groups. The main advantage of assigning students to groups is that you can ensure a mix of native languages, a balanced number of males and females, and so forth. You may form groups according to:

1. **Native language:** If students are working with others who speak a different native language, they will have to rely on English for communication.

2. **Ability levels:** The purpose of forming heterogeneous groups — mixing strong, average, and weak students in each group — is to encourage stronger students to help the weaker ones. You may also want to group the students homogeneously at times — stronger students together, average students together, and weaker students together. The advantage of this arrangement is that the stronger students may have to work harder in a more evenly matched discussion group. Average and weak students, too, can benefit from this arrangement since they cannot rely on the stronger students to carry on or to guide the discussion. These students often rise to the occasion, realizing that they themselves have total responsibility for making the discussion successful.

3. **Random sample:** One way to ensure a random mix of students is to use a numbering system. For example, imagine that you have 24 students in your class. If you want four students in each group, divide 24 by four. This gives you six. This means that the students should count off by six, — "one, two, three, four, five six, one, two, three, four, five, six, one, two, etc." until everyone has a number from one to six. Then, all the number ones form a group, all the number twos form another group, and so forth. This method prevents students from always forming groups with their friends or with those sitting near them. Another method of random selection is to write each student's name on an index card. Shuffle these cards and then choose four or five cards from the pile, depending on the number of people you want in each group. The students whose names are written on the cards will then form a group. This method adds an element of surprise to the class and ensures a constantly changing mix of students.

4. **Friendship/proximity:** You can let the students organize themselves informally into groups. Students can organize groups with their friends or with those sitting near them. The problem with this method, of course, is that some students may be ignored or left out when groups

are formed. Also, students may get into the habit of sitting with the same people.

To add variety to class, you may want to try all four methods of organizing groups.

E. Setting Time Limits

Setting time limits for activities requires a delicate balance between control and flexibility. Time limits are important because students are more likely to stay on task if they know that they have a limited amount of time in which to complete an activity. At the same time, it is difficult to know in advance exactly how long an activity will take. The best way to handle this is to inform students of approximate time limits in advance. As you circulate, you can notice how the groups are progressing and modify the time accordingly. If students are actively and enthusiastically engaged in an activity, you can extend the time limits. If an activity seems to be fizzling, you can stop it immediately. Basically, when you notice that one or two groups are near completion, you can announce a three, four, or five minute warning to give the other groups a chance to complete the activity. At times, you may have to stop an activity before all the groups have finished. Generally, it is better to stop an activity a bit too soon than to let it drag on too long.

F. Dealing with Groups that Finish Early

A common problem with group work is that one or two groups may finish much earlier than the others. When a group finishes early, your first step is to make sure that the group has thoughtfully and successfully completed the activity as assigned. For instance, have they written the answers in the book? Have they listed reasons? Have they reached agreement? If everything is in order, then you need to be prepared to provide a further task for the group. Ideally, this task should be related to the activity they have just completed. Some of the following tasks may be possible, depending on the type of activity completed:

- If group members have reached agreement on a group position with supporting reasons, have them develop reasons supporting the opposite (or different) position.

- Group members can prepare a written group report to hand in that explains the group position with supporting reasons on one of the issues explained in the activity.

14

- Each group member can write a few sentences to hand in that explains his or her personal opinion on one of the issues presented in the activity.

- If the group has provided a list of reasons to support a particular point of view, they can put these reasons in order of importance.

- The group reporter can rehearse his or her report of the group's results.

G. Providing Feedback

Be sure to include time for some type of feedback after each activity. Feedback is important because it provides students with a sense of closure as well as achievement. One type of feedback is contained within many of the activities — a sharing of results. After working on an activity with a partner or in a group, students are generally eager to share and/or compare their ideas with those of the other groups.

Another type of feedback for a group activity focuses on the process of group decision making. After a group activity, you might ask each group a question or two:

- Did all group members take an active part in reaching the final decision?

- Did any particular group member or members have a strong influence on the final decision? If so, how?

- How did you reach a final decision: through consensus, majority rule, leader decision, or what?

A third type of feedback focuses on accuracy. After some (but not all) activities, you may want to deal with a few grammar, vocabulary, or pronunciation errors you heard during the activity.

H. Assigning Roles

Initially, when you assign students to certain groups, you may want to assign the role of leader to one of the stronger students. It is important, however, to rotate this role so that all students get a chance to act as leader. Of course, groups can also be allowed to choose their own leaders; however, students may tend to keep choosing the same people to be leaders instead of rotating the position.

IV. DISCUSSION TROUBLESHOOTING GUIDE

You may find unexpected problems developing during some of the group discussion activities. The main rule to remember is — relax! You aren't expected to know all of the answers or solve all of the problems. You should encourage your students to take initiative, to take responsibility for their own learning. Make the class a team effort. If something goes wrong with a discussion, let the students figure out what happened and then develop strategies for dealing with the problem. The way to push students to take this responsibility is to make a habit of saying, "What do you think happened in this discussion? Did everyone participate? Were there any problems? What can you do so these problems don't happen in future discussions?" The evaluation forms included in the text should help guide you and the students in analyzing different aspects of the group discussion process.

The following is a list of problems that you may encounter in group discussions in your class. Don't worry. You won't encounter all of these problems, at least not all at once. Some suggestions are included to guide you in dealing with these situations.

A. Classroom Management

1. **Students waste time getting into groups.**

   a. Students seem to move more quickly if the teacher is standing up and moving around the class. Especially at the beginning of the course, you might help the students physically move the seats so they understand what kind of seating arrangement you want.

   b. Before asking students to move, be sure to give them clear instructions so they know exactly what you expect them to do.

   c. Set short time limits for pair or group work since students often get organized faster if they realize that they have a lot to do in a limited time.

2. **Students use their native language in discussion groups.**

   a. As much as possible, group students with different native languages together.

16

b.   Monitor language use by moving from group to group during activities.

c.   Ask students to do self-evaluations. During an activity, students have a sheet of paper in front of them and a pencil in hand. Every time they say something in English, they must put a check on the paper. At the end of the activity, students can report the number of times they spoke their native language.

d.   Assign observers keep a record of students who use their native language. These observers do not have to "tattle" to the teacher, but they should remind speakers to rely on English during the discussion.

e.   If students use their native language only occasionally to sort out a problem, then that is not a real problem. However, students should be encouraged to develop strategies to deal with problems and ask each other for help in English.

3.   Student ability varies widely.

a.   Encourage stronger students to help weaker students.

b.   Vary the groups. Sometimes organize groups so that each one consists of a mix of both strong and weak students. At other times, put all the weak students together, the average students together, and the strong students together. See which kind of grouping works best with your particular class.

B.   Participation/Interaction

1.   Instead of interacting (agreeing, disagreeing, asking questions, etc.), group members simply present one of their own ideas each time they have a chance to speak.

or

2.   Group members do not seem to be listening to each other. Their comments do not relate to preceding comments made by other students.

or

3.   The discussion ends quickly after each participant has given his or her opinion. The group does not attempt to reach an agreement on the best solution to the problem.

a. Review all of the functions that have been taught so far in order to encourage participants to make different kinds of contributions to the discussion. Ask the students: "What kinds of things can you do during the discussion besides giving your opinion and making a suggestion?" [Answer: agreeing, disagreeing, asking questions, getting further information, asking for clarification, comparing, etc.]

b. If videotaping facilities are available, make a videotape of student discussions. You can use these tapes to analyze group interaction. Videotape is especially useful since you can pause the tape to have students analyze the interaction.

c. When students are participating in a discussion with observers, have the observers keep a record of the different functions they hear the speakers use. This can help make students aware of how limited a range of language functions they are using.

4. **Fluent speakers dominate the discussion.**

   a. Elicit/discuss ways that group members can interrupt a speaker who is dominating the discussion. Refer to "Taking Turns" in the Communication Skills section of Unit 4.

   b. Elicit/discuss specific ways that group members can control members who are talking too much. Refer to "Leading a Group Discussion" in the Communication Skills section of Unit 6.

   c. Elicit/discuss ways that strong students can bring others into the discussion. Emphasize that they can also include others by asking questions, getting further information, asking for examples, asking for clarification, etc.

   d. Elicit/discuss reasons for including all group members in the decision-making process.
      • To make the best decision, the group needs input from all of the members.
      • Group discussions are a team effort, so all group members should do their best to make the discussion successful.

5. **Weak or shy students do not participate or participate only a little in the activity.**

    a. Try mixing the discussion groups so that sometimes the group members are of mixed abilities — strong and weak students together — to see whether the strong students can help the weak ones. Other times try putting all weak or quiet students together in a group to see whether they feel more secure and less intimidated that way. You may be quite surprised by the positive results of putting all the quiet students together.

    b. When individuals are especially weak, ask them to concentrate on one or two specific ways of improving their performance. Tell them, for example, "Try to ask other group members at least two questions," or "Try to speak two times without waiting to be asked."

    c. Keep the classroom atmosphere relaxed and non-threatening. If students are to be graded on their speaking skills, postpone grading until students have a chance to gain confidence and feel comfortable about participating in a group discussion. Give students time to learn some of the speaking skills presented in the book so that they can be graded on achievement rather than on general proficiency.

    d. Encourage strong speakers to include quiet group members.

    e. Always encourage students by giving positive reinforcement. Stress how much improvement they have made (if true). If students in a discussion group are especially weak, try to evaluate the discussion in general terms rather than singling out individuals for comment. Keep in mind how vulnerable weak or shy students may be to criticism.

    f. It may help to talk to especially weak or shy students individually. Try to find out if there is any particular problem that is preventing them from participating. If so, you can help them develop strategies for dealing with the particular problem outside of class.

19

6. Participants fail to take initiative.

    a.   Make it clear that it is each person's own responsibility to participate actively in the discussion. Participants should not wait for someone to include them or ask them questions before contributing their ideas.

    b.   Elicit/discuss ways that students can interrupt and get a point into the discussion. Refer to "Taking Turns" in the Communication Skills section of Unit 4.

C. Accuracy

1. Students do not have control of necessary grammatical structures to express their ideas clearly.

    a.   Keep a written record of the grammar errors students make as they are participating in activities or making presentations. Pay particular attention to those errors that interfere with communication. After the discussion, you can go over the most important mistakes. Of course, it is not necessary to identify the students who made each error.

    b.   Plan grammar lessons to work on language problems that you have identified during discussions or presentations. Common grammar errors include verb tense usage, question forms, word order, modals, conditionals, use of articles, and comparison forms.

    c.   You may want to use a grammar book such as *Understanding and Using English Grammar* by Betty Schrampfer Azar (Englewood Cliffs, New Jersey: Prentice Hall Regents, 1989) to supplement speaking practice.

    d.   Make an audio or video recording of a discussion. Play back short segments of the recording for the class to analyze in terms of grammatical accuracy. Stop the tape after you hear an error. Ask the class to identify and then correct each error. Of course, you can also stop the tape after a correct utterance to make sure the students can recognize a correct sentence.

e.   Make a written transcript of a segment of a discussion that you have taped. As a class, students can begin to identify and correct grammatical errors. Students can then be divided into small groups to continue this activity.

2. **Students lack the necessary vocabulary to express their ideas.**

    a.   Discuss the subject or situation for a minute or two so that students understand the general subject. Before groups begin a particular activity, you may want to try a class activity of brainstorming or mapping vocabulary words related to the subject under discussion. You can write these words on the board for student reference.

    b.   Before students participate in a group activity, try to anticipate words that they might need in order to discuss that particular topic. Elicit or present these words before the discussion, making sure that students know what they mean and how to pronounce them correctly.

    c.   As you listen to discussion groups, pay attention to the words that students search for or need to know in order to express their ideas more precisely. Keep a list of these useful vocabulary words to go over with students. You may write them on the board so that students can keep a record of them or you may regularly hand out photocopied lists of vocabulary words that the students are responsible for. You might also give occasional quizzes on these words to encourage students to study them.

D. Use of Expressions

1. **Students need to use certain expressions or discussion techniques before they are covered in the book.**

    It is not necessary to cover the expressions in the order that they are presented in the textbook. Feel free to introduce the information in the way that you think will help your students the most. When you see that students will benefit from knowing certain expressions, present them immediately.

2. **Participants make no attempt to use the expressions taught in the course.**

    a. Review the expressions that you have already covered in class. If students seem to have difficulty remembering the different expressions, you might spend a few minutes of each class reviewing the expressions for a few different functions. For example, you can ask: "What expressions can you use for giving a suggestion?" or "What expressions can you use to disagree politely with someone?" When a student gives an answer, ask the class: "What else can you say?"

    b. You might want to have students write out the expressions for practice. Give students short in-class practice at regular intervals by choosing two or three functions (such as giving an opinion, disagreeing, clarifying, etc.) to write on the board. Then tell the students: "Write down all the expressions you can remember for these particular functions."

3. **Participants use expressions inaccurately (incorrect grammatical usage) or inappropriately (in the wrong context).**

    a. Make a note of the errors you hear during activities so that you can deal with them at the end of the discussion or in a future lesson.

    b. Have observers keep a record of the expressions used by participants. You might assign each observer to note the expressions used by one particular student, so different observers concentrate on different participants. Observers should also decide whether each expressions was used correctly or not. Observers can then include their observations as part of the evaluation. This type of individual evaluation should be postponed, though, until students are comfortable enough not to be threatened by such individual attention.

E. Student Attitude

1. **Students seem overly sensitive to suggestions for improvement.**

   a. When evaluating students, even informally, be positive. Always praise strong points before mentioning any weaknesses. Also get student observers into the habit of discussing strengths before weaknesses.

   b. Do not mention every mistake that individuals make. This can be quite discouraging to the students. Instead, concentrate on only one or two different suggestions for improvement.

2. **Students do not seem interested in the situations presented in the activities.**

   a. You and/or the students can adapt the details to suit local circumstances.

   b. Students can also develop their own topics based on personal experience, articles in the newspaper, local business situations, or problems in their own company or business.

F. Group Leadership

1. **The group leader dominates the discussion.**

   a. Elicit/discuss responsibilities of the group leader. Refer to "Leading a Group Discussion" in the Communication Skills section of Unit 6.

   b. Point out that leaders have an obligation to ensure the balanced participation of all members.

2. **The group leader fails to carry out leadership responsibilities.**

   a. Elicit/discuss the functions of a group leader.

   b. Point out that the discussion is a team effort. Group members other than the leader can assume some of the leadership functions such as including quiet members, controlling talkative participants, returning to the subject, etc.

V. ORAL PRESENTATIONS

A. Dealing with Stage Fright

This text has been designed to involve students in numerous pair and group activities before having them give class presentations. Thus, by the time students have to make presentations, they should feel relatively comfortable speaking in class. It is natural, however, that students will feel more nervous about giving presentations. The information in "Building Confidence" in the Communication Skills section of Unit 3 provides specific suggestions to help students deal with stage fright.

Before having students give presentations to the class, encourage them to discuss their feelings of nervousness. They may feel slightly better when they realize that others share their same fears. Ask questions, such as:

- Have you ever given a talk or a presentation to a group or to a class? If so, who was your audience? What did you talk about? How did you feel?
- Why do people feel so nervous when they have to speak to a group?
- What can people do to lessen their feelings of nervousness?

In general, the best way to deal with stage fright is to provide students with numerous opportunities to speak — in pairs, in groups, and to the class. Be sure to emphasize that the best way for students to feel more confident when giving presentations is by being completely prepared.

B. Preparing for Presentations

The text includes a number of activities to help students develop appropriate topics for class presentations. However, you may still find that students experience some difficulty with this task. For this reason, you may want to require students to get your approval of their topics soon after the presentations are assigned. If you have students hand in two or three possible topics, you can select the best one. By approving student topics, you can eliminate unsuitable presentations and avoid the problem of multiple presentations on the same topic. You may find it helpful to keep a record of the topics you approve for each student to make sure that students do not change their topics without consulting you.

You should emphasize the importance of preparation and practice by scheduling class time for some preparatory activities, especially at the beginning of the course.

1. **In advance:** Assign students to have outlines of their presentations prepared two class periods before they are officially scheduled to be presented in class.

2. **First class period:** Students work in small groups to discuss their outlines. They can work together to make any necessary changes or revisions in these outlines. At this stage, you can circulate to provide suggestions for revisions. Homework for the next class period is for students to bring in revised outlines plus presentation notes on index cards.

3. **Second class period:** Students exchange and discuss their note cards in pairs or groups, referring to "Speaking from Notes" in the Communication Skills section of Unit 3. If notes do not meet specifications, students can start rewriting them in class. You should continue circulating to comment on strengths and weaknesses of the revised outlines and the note cards.

You may also want to have students hand in their presentation notes after they give each presentation.

C. Scheduling Presentations

Scheduling presentations is a balancing act that includes several important considerations:

1. **How much total class time do you want to devote to presentations?**

   You may want to adjust the time limits indicated in the presentation activities according to the amount of class time available. You may also want to consider dividing the class so two or more students can give presentations simultaneously to groups rather than one-by-one to the entire class.

2. **How much time are you planning to allow for each presentation?**

   You may want to include a limited amount of time for a question-and-answer session after each presentation. If so, add two minutes (or so) to the time allotted for each presentation. Here again, though, be sure to observe strict time limits or you will end up spending much more time than you had planned on class presentations.

3. **What is your and/or the students' attention span? If your class meets for two-hour sessions or double class periods, can you (or do you want to) sit through two straight hours of presentations?**

   In this case, you may want to spread out the presentations over a number of class periods, mixing in pair or group activities to add variety to each class.

4. **How will you determine speaking order?**

   One of the most common ways to determine speaking order is to have students draw numbers. You can then give students one minute to exchange numbers if they wish. After determining the speaking order, make a list of the students in the order that they will be speaking. With this list, you can remind students of their order, thus helping speed things along.

D. Managing Time

Although class presentations can be very time consuming, careful time management can make the process reasonably efficient. Be strict about observing time limits; otherwise, presentations will consume an inordinate amount of class time and student interest may start to dwindle. Of course, you need to inform the students in advance about the importance of meeting the time limits — both minimum and maximum. Presentations that run much shorter than the minimum or longer than the maximum reveal a lack of planning and rehearsing. One common problem is that many speakers tend to run over time, so you need to be prepared to deal with this in advance. What can you do?

- Emphasize how important it is for students to plan their time carefully. By rehearsing their presentations in advance, students will be able to add or delete information so that each presentation meets the time limits.

- For the first presentation or two, remind students of the time limits when the presentation is assigned, when they are preparing, and on the day of the presentations. Tell them that they cannot speak longer than the allotted time.

- Be strict (even heartless) about observing the stated time limits. An electronic timer (that marks seconds as well as minutes) is especially useful for timing presentations. Have a student volunteer set the timer to the maximum time limit. When the beeper/buzzer goes off, the speaker must conclude in a sentence or two. If the presentation ends before the timer beeps, the student volunteer can tell you the time remaining. If you don't have a timer, one of the students will probably have a watch that can be used as a timer or simply use a watch with a second hand. At the end of each presentation, ask the student volunteer for "Time?" and then mark it on the evaluation form.

• Keep speakers moving at a fast pace. As one speaker sits down, the next speaker should be moving to the front. You can help keep things moving by reminding students of the order: "Okay, it's Mary's turn, and then John is next."

E. Evaluating Presentations

You will find presentation evaluation forms for Units 3 and 5 in Appendix A of the text. You may use these forms for any other presentation assignments you give students. When you assign a presentation, be sure to review the appropriate evaluation form with the students. Discuss the criteria in advance so students know exactly what is expected of them as they are preparing their presentations. As much as possible, fill out the evaluation forms while students are giving their presentations. Let students know in advance that you will be taking notes while they are speaking (if you plan to do so). This advance notice may help lessen their anxieties that you are writing down all of their mistakes. In general, the more detailed your comments are, the more helpful the feedback will be for the students. Of course, your feedback should focus on strong points as well as weaknesses (tactfully referred to as "areas for improvement"). More specific information about evaluation procedures is presented in the following Evaluation section.

VI.   EVALUATION

A. Using Student Self-Evaluations

In a learner-centered course, students should take responsibility for monitoring and assessing their own performance. Thus, self-evaluation has been built into this course through the activities in the Learning Strategies section of each unit. The purpose of these activities is to focus the students' attention on their progress in learning English so they know where to focus their efforts.

If you wish, you can include an element of self-evaluation in many activities in this text. Before you begin an activity, write one, two, or three questions on the board, focusing on areas that you feel are in need of improvement. At the same time, if necessary, provide an appropriate key for students to use in answering these questions. Some possible types of keys include:

- + = very good; ✓ = satisfactory; — = needs more practice

- + = frequently; ✓ = sometimes; — = almost never

- + = yes; ✓ = partially; — = no

When the activity is completed, students can discuss their answers in small groups or as a class. Some possible questions to use for this purpose are:

FOR PAIR OR GROUP ACTIVITIES

- Did you speak only English?
- Did you look directly at each speaker?
- Did you take an equal part in the discussion?
- Did you take initiative by making comments or asking questions?
- Did you encourage the other speaker(s) verbally and/or nonverbally?
- Did you use new expressions from this unit?
- Did you take turns appropriately?
- Did you ask questions?
- Did you include other speakers?
- Did you stay on the subject?

FOR PRESENTATIONS

- Did you maintain eye contact with your audience?
- Did you speak loudly and clearly?
- Did you speak in a natural, conversational manner?
- Did your introduction gain the audience's attention?
- Did you use clear transitions to connect your ideas?
- Did you have a strong conclusion?

B. Using Peer Evaluations

The purpose of peer evaluation is to encourage students to learn from one another and to rely less on the teacher as an authority figure. By evaluating one another, students gain a clearer understanding of the criteria used to evaluate successful communication. Peer evaluation is built into the course through the presence of student observers in a number of activities. You can also encourage peer evaluation by having students occasionally complete the evaluation forms in Appendix A of the text. To do this, photocopy these forms for classroom use and then assign one or more students to observe each group or each speaker. You might want to have the student evaluators hand in the forms so you can review them before giving them to the speakers.

You may want to have students observe discussions more often than the activities indicate. In this case, hand out an observation form or write specific questions on the board for the observers to focus on. In fact, you can use questions very similar to those included in the preceding section on Self-Evaluation, changing "you" to "the speaker." You may also develop further activities such as the following:

PEER EVALUATION ACTIVITY

1. Work as a group. Review the following expressions that speakers use to agree and disagree. Can you think of any other expressions to add to the list?

AGREE | DISAGREE

That's right.   I don't really agree with you.
I agree with you.   I'm not sure I agree with you.
I think so, too.   I can you point, but . . . .
I completely agree.   I see what you mean, but . . .

2. During the group discussion, the observer makes a list of all the expressions the speakers use to agree and/or disagree.

3. At the end of discussion, the observer shares his/her results with the group.

C. Evaluating Students

Your evaluation of individual, pair, and group activities can take many forms: oral feedback, written evaluations, letter grades, pass/fail grades, and so forth. Whatever method you use, here are some general guidelines in evaluating students:

1. When providing any type of feedback or evaluation, always mention strengths as well as weaknesses.

2. If a student is especially weak, focus on only one or two areas for improvement in order not to completely discourage him or her.

3. While written feedback is always useful, students may feel even more anxious about speaking if they know they will be graded on their performance. Therefore, postpone grading for several weeks (if possible) to give students a chance to practice, build their skills, and increase their confidence.

4. Use the evaluation forms in Appendix A of the text to provide detailed, constructive feedback that focuses on strengths as well as areas for improvement.

D. Using the Evaluation Forms

The evaluation forms in Appendix A of the text focus on different aspects of conversation, discussion, and presentation skills. Each evaluation form includes detailed communicative criteria to provide a rating scale for evaluation. Your detailed comments, suggestions, and questions on this form can provide each student with a great deal of useful, specific feedback.

Before using these forms, review the criteria with the students so they know exactly what is expected of them. By establishing the criteria early in the course, you will give students a clear understanding of the course objectives. These evaluation forms offer you and the students several important advantages:

- They provide students with specific feedback they can use to improve their performance.

- They provide you with specific information concerning students' strengths and weaknesses to guide you in planning future lessons.

- They can help you keep track of students' progress and serve as a solid basis for assigning grades (if necessary).

When you plan to evaluate an activity, photocopy blank forms for you and/or student observers to use. Then, after the discussion or presentation, photocopy the completed forms so that you can hand one back to each student and also keep one for your records.

E. Adapting the Evaluation Forms

You may find that the breakdown of categories on some of the evaluation forms does not reflect the exact areas of conversation, discussion, or presentation skills that you want to emphasize. In this case, you can redesign the form to suit the needs of your class. A standard size sheet of paper will provide more space for your comments. In modifying, dropping, or adding criteria, be sure to keep the descriptions based on communicative principles. Also, keep the number of categories limited in order to facilitate using the form. The more categories you include, the more separate decisions you have to make regarding each student's performance. Once you have designed a suitable form to fit standard size paper, you can use it as a master to make as many photocopies as you need. As you use the form, you can see whether the format fits your needs and then make any necessary adjustments.

F. Examining the Pros and Cons of Grading

Many teachers feel uncomfortable and apprehensive about grading speaking/listening skills. Some common complaints about giving grades in a speaking/listening course are:

- Grades are too subjective and unreliable.

- Grades unnecessarily increase student anxiety.

- Grades seem to measure students' general proficiency rather than their achievement in a particular class. Students in the same class often have widely differing levels of speaking/listening skills when they begin the course. Thus, some students seem to have an unfair advantage over others from the beginning of the term.

- Grades may unfairly reflect students' personalities. Outgoing, confident students seem to have a natural advantage over shy, insecure students, even if they are at the same level of language proficiency.

- Grades may unfairly reflect cultural/educational backgrounds. Students coming from educational systems that encourage active student participation seem to have a natural advantage over those coming from traditional systems that encourage passivity and acceptance of the teacher's authority.

- Grades may reflect other factors that students cannot control. For example, students from some language backgrounds have much greater difficulty with English pronunciation/intonation than students from other language backgrounds. Here again, some students seem to have a natural advantage over others.

Of course, other teachers focus more on the advantages of grading speaking/listening skills:

- The use of a limited number of clearly delineated criteria makes grading less subjective. Furthermore, even subjective grades are useful since they reflect the teacher's judgment, intuition, and experience.

- Grades reward students for progress and motivate them to study. Many students are used to being motivated by grades. They may put more effort into acquiring a skill if they know they will be graded on it.

- Some students do not take a skill seriously unless they are graded on it.

- Grades generally provide a measure of a student's ability that students and other teachers can understand.

G. Using the Evaluation Forms to Assign Grades

If you plan to assign grades, you can use the evaluation forms in the following ways:

- Use symbols (+, ✓, and —) on the form to indicate each speaker's or each group's strengths and weaknesses, and then give an overall impressionistic grade. Write more specific comments, suggestions, or questions to provide as much detailed information as possible to each speaker. In fact, this is the author's preferred method.

- Assign a numerical value to each symbol. For example, a plus (+) equals 3 points, a check (✓) equals 2 points, and a minus (—) equals 1 point. After completing the evaluation form, add up the speaker's or group's points out of the total number of possible points. For example, if you use all the categories in the Presentation Evaluation Form for Unit 3, you have a total of 30 possible points. The range of possible scores is then from 10 to 30 points. You can then set up a scale, based on the grading system you use. One possible grading scale might be:

A = 26-30 points   D = 13-15 points

B = 21-25 points   F = 10-12 points

C = 16-20 points

Of course, this scale is just one possible way of sorting out the numerical scores.

H. Determining Course Grades

If you have to give course grades, your method of grading will depend to a great extent on your philosophy of teaching and grading as well as the demands of your program. You need to find a grading method that you feel is practical, fair, and efficient. Your method of grading must also meet any administrative guidelines or requirements. In any case, whatever grading method you use, be sure to inform students at the beginning of the course exactly how their course grades will be determined.

In fact, there are countless ways to determine course grades in a speaking/listening course. Most methods generally involve your keeping copies of all completed evaluation forms and/or keeping careful attendance records. If you are able to determine your own method of grading, you might consider the following possibilities:

1. **Impression grading**: You can use your judgment and experience to give each student a final grade that reflects his/or her overall speaking/listening ability. To refresh your memory of each student's progress in the course, you should refer to the completed evaluation forms. The final grade may reflect performance, effort, or a combination of the two.

2. **Participation/preparation/attendance**: Grades based on these criteria encourage participation, decrease anxiety about performance, and motivate students to attend regularly. With this method, however, you need to keep careful records of student attendance. You also need to keep a record in your grade book of student performance on selected group activities and individual presentations, using a plus (+), check (✓), minus (—), zero (0) rating system to indicate the level of student preparation or participation.

   The main disadvantage of this method is in dealing with student absences. You may find yourself involved in the sticky issue of excused versus unexcused absences. Some students may take up a considerable amount of time trying to convince you to change an unexcused to an excused absence. You also face other problems. How do you deal with a student who misses a number of classes because of sickness? How do you know whether a student is really sick or has simply decided to take a day off? The best way to deal with this problem is to allow each student two or three absences (or whatever you feel is a fair number) for whatever reason without any penalty. This will save you from discussing or debating every absence with students who are overly concerned about your grading policy. You can then deal individually with students who miss more than the stated number of days.

3. **Performance**: With this method, you grade selected activities and assigned presentations. You can then average these grades, preferably giving more weight to the grades in the later part of the course. The reason for this is that the course is cumulative, so the students' performance at the end of the course more accurately reflects what they have learned. One way to weight grades is to have a final graded group activity and a final graded individual presentation, each worth 20 percent or 30 percent of the final grade.

4. **Averaging**: You can determine a student's course grade by averaging (1) participation/preparation/effort and (2) performance. For example, you might count performance as 50 percent and participation, preparation, and effort as the other 50 percent.

5. **Percentage breakdown**: You may want to develop your own personal method to suit your approach to the course. For example, some teachers design quizzes to test the students' progress in listening comprehension and then include these grades. The following is just one of many possible ways to determine a final course grade:

Attendance/participation:	40%
Midterm listening quiz:	10%
Midterm speaking activity:	10%
Final group activity:	10%
Final listening exam:	15%
Final presentation:	15%
	100%

FINAL GRADES:

A = 90% - 100%
B = 80% - 89%
C = 70% - 79%
D = 60% - 69%
F = 50% and below

6. **Benefit of the doubt**: At the beginning of the course, you assume that everyone in the class is a good student who deserves a B. As the course progresses, most students will stay at this level. However, some students may clearly rise above this level while others may fall below it. You then give a grade of A to those students who rise above the level, impressing you with strong speaking/listening skills, excellent attendance, noticeable preparation, and/or extra effort. You give a grade of C to those students who fall below the level due to very weak skills, irregular attendance, and/or little effort. You can give grades of D or F to students with very poor speaking/listening skills, excessive absences, lack of preparation, and/or no effort to improve. Clearly, this is not a very "scientific" method and may not be suitable for many classes. Since this method of grading seems more intuitive, it may be hard to explain or to justify to students. It is included here, however, for better or worse, because a number of experienced teachers have "admitted" to using this method.

VII. ADDITIONAL CLASSROOM ACTIVITIES

A. Breaking the Ice

This activity is appropriate if students in your class have several different native languages. This is a good ice-breaking activity to help students get used to speaking in front of the class.

PROCEDURE:

1. List some or all of the following on the board:

    a. Hello.
    b. Good morning.
    c. Good afternoon.
    d. How are you?
    e. I'm fine.
    f. What's your name?
    g. Where do you come from?
    h. I come from the U.S.
    i. What do you do?
    j. I'm a student.
    k. Good-bye. See you tomorrow.

2. Each student chooses several of the sentences or questions from the list. [Students who speak the same language should choose different items.] Each student then goes to the front of the room, writes the sentence or question in his or her native language (with any appropriate changes) on the board, and then teaches it to the class.

B. Answering Questions

Take advantage of every minute of class time. The following is a list of miscellaneous questions — not intended to be taken very seriously. If you have a few minutes free before class ends, go around the room to have each student give a quick answer to one of the following:

- What's your favorite meal?
- What kinds of things do you like to do with your family?
- What's your favorite day of the week? Why?

- What's your favorite time of day? Why?
- What's the best way to travel — independently or in a group?
- What's the ideal number of children to have? How many boys/girls?
- What's the ideal age for men to get married? For women to get married?
- How would you spend $1,000?
- What are the advantages of being a sports star such as Michael Jordan? What are the disadvantages?
- If you could change one thing in this classroom, what would it be?
- If you could meet anyone living in the world today, who would you meet? Why?
- How often did you get into trouble when you were a child? What kind of trouble?
- What brand of toothpaste do you use? Why do you use that particular brand?

C. Giving Impromptu Talks

The purpose of impromptu talks is to get students used to speaking informally in front of the class. With little or no preparation, have some or all of the students take turns giving a brief talk on one of the following. You may want to set a very short time limit for some of these talks:

IF STUDENTS ARE FROM DIFFERENT COUNTRIES:

1. Describe your hometown.

   PROCEDURE: Elicit/discuss the kind of information students should include:

   a. name of city or town
   b. part of the country where it is located
   c. population
   d. main businesses or industries
   e. types of entertainment
   f. interesting places people should see or visit
   g. reasons that it is or is not a good place to live

37

2. Describe a festival or holiday in your country.

   PROCEDURE: Elicit/discuss the kind of information students should include:

   a. reasons this holiday is important
   b. ways that people celebrate this holiday
   c. special food, special clothes, special activities
   d. reasons that you like this holiday

3. Discuss an important custom in your country, such as the way people celebrate engagements, weddings, births, etc.

4. Describe an important event in your country's history.

5. Describe the life of a famous person in your country who is no longer living. What made this person famous?

IF STUDENTS ARE FROM THE SAME COUNTRY:

1. Present the summary of a story in the newspaper or a magazine.

2. Explain the plot of a television program, a movie, or a book.

3. Get a non-news popular magazine in English, such as *Reader's Digest*, *Sports Illustrated*, *Popular Mechanics*, *Glamour*, etc. Present a two- to three-minute summary of an article that interests you.

D. Giving Advice

This activity is an old one, but still seems popular with students. Select problems from personal advice columns, such as "Dear Abby," that you think your students will find interesting. Read or distribute copies of the problem (not including the answer) to students. Students then work in pairs or groups to develop a solution to the problem. You can then read the advice provided in the column to the students and have them compare their answers. Be sure to emphasize that the answer in the newspaper is not the "correct" answer.

E. Retelling a Story

The purpose of this activity is to have students retell a story several times to see how much the story changes as it is told to several different people. The story included in this activity is a rather strange event (true!) taken from the newspaper. As students retell the story, it can get even stranger, so students should have fun with this activity. Of course, you can also choose your own story to replace the one presented here.

1. Prepare for this activity by reading these instructions and the story. Adapt the story, if you feel it is necessary, to avoid unknown vocabulary words.

2. Give a brief explanation of this activity and select four students to send out of the room. These four students should be relatively confident and/or outgoing since weak or shy students may feel uncomfortable if they feel others are laughing at their mistakes.

3. With these four students out of the room, read or tell the story to the class. Students may not take any notes, but they can ask questions to make sure they understand the story. Students should be prepared to retell this story in as much detail as possible without notes and without help from you.

4. Now call one of the four students, Student 1, back into the room. Choose a student in class to retell the story from memory (with no help of any kind) to Student 1. Student 1 may ask questions, but cannot write anything down. Only the storyteller and Student 1 should speak.

5. Now have Student 2 come back into the room. Student 1 must tell Student 2 the story from memory, with no help from anyone else. Then call Student 3 in and have Student 2 retell the story to him or her. This step is repeated with Student 4. Finally, have Student 4 tell the story to the class. You should then read the original story to see how different the stories are.

6. Work as a class. Discuss the following:
   • How did the story change as each speaker told it?
   • How different was the story Speaker 4 told from the story told by the teacher?
   • What problems did the observers notice as the story was passed from one student to another?

STORY:

Today I'd like to tell you a true story about an unusual bus trip that I read about recently. The name of the bus driver was John Massenberg. John was a new driver for a bus company and it was time for him to make his first long-distance trip by himself, without another driver supervising him. This long-distance trip was an overnight drive from Atlanta, Georgia to Tallahassee, Florida — a distance of about 400 miles. After driving for a few hours, John began talking to the passengers — which was against the bus company rules. He started complaining about driving at night and he told everyone how tired he felt. A few minutes later, he was so worried about falling asleep that he asked the passengers to help keep him awake. After a while, he was so tired that he asked the passengers if one of them would volunteer to drive the bus. Of course, none of the passengers wanted that responsibility. So, when no one volunteered to drive, John pulled the bus off the highway, told the passengers he was quitting his job, sat in one of the passenger seats, and immediately went to sleep. While he was sleeping, one of the passengers, an off-duty policeman, decided to start driving the bus toward their destination. After about thirty miles, the bus driver, John, woke up and took over the driving. Fortunately, the bus arrived safely, but unfortunately for John, bus company officials fired him immediately. The officials told the passengers that this was the first time they had had such a strange problem with one of their bus drivers.

VIII. ANSWERS TO LISTENING AND PRONUNCIATION PRACTICE ACTIVITIES

A. Unit 1

UNIT 1, ACTIVITY 1
A. How do you spell that?
B. Sorry, I didn't hear what you said.
C. Excuse me?
D. Could you please repeat your question?
E. I'm sorry, but I'm not sure I understand your question.
F. Pardon?
G. I'm sorry. Could you please speak a little more slowly?
H. Would you mind repeating your question?

UNIT 1, ACTIVITY 2
A. teacher—student
B. classmates
C. strangers
D. classmates
E. employer—employee
F. employer—employee
G. teacher—student
H. co-workers
I. co-workers
J. strangers

UNIT 1, ACTIVITY 9

1. 2	5. 2	9. 3	13. 1
2. 3	6. 3	10. 1	14. 4
3. 4	7. 5	11. 4	15. 1
4. 1	8. 2	12. 2	16. 5

UNIT 1, ACTIVITY 11

1. pre(sent)
2. re(cord)
3. (con)trast
4. con(duct)
5. (in)crease
6. ob(ject)
7. (prog)ress
8. in(sult)
9. (sub)ject
10. (prod)uce
11. per(mit)
12. de(crease)

41

UNIT 1, ACTIVITY 12

1. at (ten) tion
2. ex (am) ple
3. un der (stand)
4. (dif) fi cult
5. in tro (duce)
6. (nec) es sary
7. mis (take)
8. re (la) tion ship
9. com pre (hen) sion
10. sit u (a) tion
11. op por (tu) ni ty
12. ac a (dem) ic
13. dis (cus) sion
14. (ques) tion
15. ap (pro) pri ate
16. pro nun ci (a) tion
17. (au) di ence
18. par (tic) i pate
19. pro (fes) sion al
20. (con) fi dent

B. Unit 2

UNIT 2, ACTIVITY 1

BRIEF RESPONSES	INFORMATION QUESTIONS
A. Oh really?	What happened?
B. You did?	What was it?
C. Three people?	Who were they?
D. Did you?	Was it hard?
E. I see.	What level are you in now?
F. Oh no!	What did you do?
G. Paris? That's great.	When does your vacation start?
H. Oh?	What company do you work for?

UNIT 2, ACTIVITY 2

A. How do you like this weather?
B. Nice day, isn't it?
C. Look at this line!
D. Hi, John. How's it going today?
E. Hello, Denise. How are you?
F. Excuse me. Do you know what time it is?

UNIT 2, ACTIVITY 3
A. Anyway, I see it's getting late.
B. Well, listen. I should be going.
C. So, I'll let you get back to work now.
D. Well, I know you're busy.

UNIT 2, ACTIVITY 14

1.	*t*	5.	*t*	9.	*id*
2.	*d*	6.	*d*	10.	*t*
3.	*t*	7.	*d*	11.	*id*
4.	*id*	8.	*d*	12.	*d*

UNIT 2, ACTIVITY 15

1.	Right	6.	Wrong
2.	Wrong	7.	Right
3.	Wrong	8.	Right
4.	Right	9.	Wrong
5.	Wrong	10.	Wrong

C. Unit 3

UNIT 3, ACTIVITY 1
A. In the Andes mountains.
B. The road was very narrow. A mountain wall went straight up on the speaker's side. On the right, the roadside dropped straight down thousands of feet into the jungle. There was no fence. The road had many dangerous curves.
C. The Amazon jungle.
D. To have enough room to get around the curve without going over the edge of the mountain.
E. It went over the edge of the mountain.
F. They moved over to the side of the bus to look out over the edge of the mountain.
G. They moved to the other side of the bus and then jumped out of their windows.
H. They helped push the bus back onto the road.
I. An earthquake and heavy rain destroyed the road.
J. Alive inside.

UNIT 3, ACTIVITY 2
A. About two years ago
B. After a while
C. When we were almost to the top of the mountain
D. At exactly the same moment
E. At that moment
F. After that
G. Then
H. Meanwhile
I. Finally
J. Two days later

UNIT 3, ACTIVITY 3
main, teacher, important, make, example, mistake, feel, learn, ideas, trouble, means, important, Finally, conversation, because, several, preparation

UNIT 3, ACTIVITY 15

1. *z*	5. *s*	9. *iz*
2. *z*	6. *s*	10. *z*
3. *s*	7. *z*	11. *iz*
4. *iz*	8. *s*	12. *iz*

UNIT 3, ACTIVITY 16

1. Wrong	6. Wrong	
2. Wrong	7. Right	
3. Right	8. Wrong	
4. Right	9. Right	
5. Wrong	10. Wrong	

D. Unit 4

UNIT 4, ACTIVITY 1
Refer to the tapescript in this manual.

UNIT 4, ACTIVITY 2

A.	Agree.	I agree with you.
B.	Disagree.	Yes, that may be true, but. . . .
C.	Disagree.	I see what you mean, but. . . .
D.	Agree.	I completely agree.
E.	Disagree.	I'm afraid I can't agree with you.

UNIT 4, ACTIVITY 3

A. Privacy
B. Excuse me for interrupting, but. . . .
   Sorry to interrupt, but. . . .
C. Excuse me, but could I just finish this one point?
D. May I say something here?
E. I guess we'll just have to agree to disagree on this subject.

UNIT 4, ACTIVITY 16

essential, reason, people, problems, control, pass, free, pay, controversy, right, obligation

E. Unit 5

UNIT 5, ACTIVITY 1

INTRODUCTION
I. Panhandlers have taken control of the city
   A. Panhandlers are everywhere
      Ex.: They're on sidewalks, in <u>parks</u>, in public buildings, and in bus stations; they stand in front of <u>shops</u> and block entrances to the subway
   B. They have become a serious social <u>problem</u>
   C. Poor and homeless people need help
   D. However, giving them money <u>is not a good way to help</u>

II. There are three reasons that people <u>should not give money</u> to panhandlers

BODY
I. Giving money does not <u>solve</u> panhandlers' real problems
   A. Many panhandlers suffer from mental illness, <u>drug</u> addiction, and alcoholism
   B. They need to go to agencies that provide long-term <u>help</u> for their problems
      Ex.: job counseling, drug and alcohol rehabilitation
   C. Giving money discourages panhandlers from trying to get <u>more permanent help</u>
   D. You make situation worse by giving money so they can buy <u>alcohol</u> and <u>drugs</u>

45

II. Giving money makes the streets more <u>frightening and dangerous</u>
  A. Giving money encourages panhandlers to continue <u>begging</u>
  B. Some panhandlers are quiet and polite, but others <u>demand</u> money
  C. Panhandlers scare people by shouting at them, <u>following</u> them, or blocking their way
  D. Pedestrians are afraid to walk down the street
  E. Some people believe panhandlers have a <u>right</u> to stand in public places asking for money
  F. However, city residents have a right to feel <u>safe</u> walking in the city

III. Many panhandlers are able to work, but they are <u>lazy</u>
  A. They don't want to work hard for low pay, so begging is an easy way to get money without working
  B. By giving money, you discourage panhandlers from <u>looking for a real job</u>
  C. Some panhandlers have signs saying they are hungry, but when you give money, they buy cigarettes, alcohol, or <u>drugs</u> instead of food
  D. You don't know which people put your money to good use

CONCLUSION
I. Panhandlers need help, but you shouldn't give money
II. Other ways to help them
  A. Donate money to an organized charity
  B. Donate your <u>time</u> by volunteering to work in a homeless shelter
  C. Write to government officials to put pressure on them to <u>provide more services and more help for homeless people</u>

UNIT 5, ACTIVITY 2
A. The speaker gains attention by describing a personal anecdote.
B. In the first place, The second reason, My third and final reason
C. In conclusion

UNIT 5, ACTIVITY 18
1. N	5. N	9. A
2. A	6. A	10. N
3. A	7. N	11. A
4. N	8. N	12. N

F. Unit 6

UNIT 6, ACTIVITY 1
A. It will give the killer what he wanted in the first place, a lot of publicity.
B. He'll be happy he's famous.
C. It makes the murder seem like entertainment.
D. The interview is like a reward for a crime.
E. It will encourage other sick people to try the same thing.
F. the author will read publicity and a lot of money.
G. People will benefit — earn money from a murder.
H. It will cause the family more pain.
I. It might help people understand what causes a person to commit such terrible crimes.
J. The speaker says that the disadvantages outweigh the advantages.

UNIT 6, ACTIVITY 2
A. I'm not sure what you mean.
B. Sorry, but I don't understand what you mean by. . . .
C. Let me see if I understand you.
D. So you mean. . . ?
E. Could you explain what you mean by. . . ?
F. Are you saying that. . . ?

UNIT 6, ACTIVITY 16
1.	A	5.	A
2.	B	6.	B
3.	A	7.	B
4.	B	8.	A

G. Unit 7

UNIT 7, ACTIVITY 1
A. 1. effectiveness
   2. practicality
   3. acceptability

B. 1. time
   2. cost
   3. effectiveness

C. 1. cost
   2. effectiveness
   3. practicality

D. 1. acceptability
   2. time
   3. cost
   4. practicality

UNIT 7, ACTIVITY 2

A. acceptability   D. effectiveness
B. practicality   E. cost
C. practicality   F. time

UNIT 7, ACTIVITY 13

1. Q   5. S   9. S   13. S
2. Q   6. Q   10. Q   14. S
3. S   7. Q   11. S   15. Q
4. Q   8. S   12. Q   16. Q

UNIT 7, ACTIVITY 15

1. R   5. R   9. F   13. R
2. R   6. F   10. F   14. R
3. F   7. R   11. F   15. R
4. R   8. F   12. F   16. F

IX. BIBLIOGRAPHY

The following books provide background information on different aspects of ethical/moral reasoning:

Arbuthnot, Jack Braeden and David Faust. (1981). *Teaching Moral Reasoning: Theory and Practice.* New York: Harper and Row, Publishers.

Bayles, Michael D. (1989). *Professional Ethics* (2nd Edition). Belmont, California: Wadsworth Publishing Company.

Beauchamp, Tom L. (1991). *Philosophical Ethics: An Introduction to Moral Philosophy.* New York: McGraw-Hill, Inc.

Beyer, Barry K. (1982). Conducting moral discussions in the classroom. In Alfred S. Alschuler (Ed.), *Values Concepts and Techniques* (Revised ed.). Washington, D.C.: National Education Association.

Bok, Sisela. (1988). The limits of confidentiality. In Joshua Halberstam (Ed.). *Virtues and Values: An Introduction to Ethics* (pp. 235-245). Englewood Cliffs, New Jersey: Prentice Hall.

Brady, F. Neil. (1990). *Ethical Managing: Rules and Results.* London: Macmillan Publishing Company.

Evans, W. Keith and Terry P. Applegate. (1982). Values decisions and the acceptability of value principles. In Alfred S. Alschuler (Ed.), *Values Concepts and Techniques* (Revised ed.). Washington, D.C.: National Education Association.

Feinberg, Joel. (1988). The scope of rights. In Joshua Halberstam (Ed.). *Virtues and Values: An Introduction to Ethics* (pp. 302-309). Englewood Cliffs, New Jersey: Prentice Hall.

Gilligan, Carol. (1982). *In a Different Voice.* Cambridge, Massachusetts: Harvard University Press.

Goodwin, H.Eugene. (1987). *Groping for Ethics in Journalism.* Ames, Iowa: Iowa State University Press.

Guy, Mary E. (1990). *Ethical Decision Making in Everyday Work Situations*. New York: Quorum Books.

Hodgson, Kent. (1992). *A Rock and a Hard Place: How to Make Ethical Business Decisions When the Choices Are Tough*. New York: American Management Association.

Kohlberg, Lawrence. (1982). The cognitive-developmental approach to moral education. In Alfred S. Alschuler (Ed.), *Values Concepts and Techniques* (Revised ed.). Washington, D.C.: National Education Association.

Morrill Richard L. (1980). *Teaching Values in College: Facilitating Development of Ethical, Moral, and Value Awareness in Students*. San Francisco, California: Jossey-Bass Publishers.

Ruggiero, Vincent Ryan. (1991). *The Art of Thinking: A Guide to Critical and Creative Thought* (3rd ed.). New York: HarperCollins Publishers.

Toffler, Barbara Ley. (1986). *Tough Choices: Managers Talk Ethics*. New York: John Wiley & Sons.

X. TAPESCRIPT

A. UNIT 1

UNIT 1, LISTENING PRACTICE, ACTIVITY 1: IDENTIFYING EXPRESSIONS

A. M1: My name is David Jenkins.
F1: Jenkins? How do you spell that?
M1: J-E-N-K-I-N-S.
F1: Oh, I see. Jenkins.

B. F2: Where were you born?
M2: Sorry, I didn't hear what you said.
F2: I asked — where were you born?
M2: Oh, I was born in New York.

C. M1: What's your native language?
F1: Excuse me?
M1: What language do you speak?
F1: Oh, I speak Spanish.

D. F2: Are you a graduate student?
M2: Could you please repeat your question?
F2: Certainly. I asked if you were a graduate or an undergraduate student.
M2: Actually, I'm a graduate student.

E. F1: What's your major?
M1: My . . . major? I'm sorry, but I'm not sure I understand your question.
F1: At the university, what subject are you studying? You know, like business, engineering, political science,. . . .
M1: Oh, right. My major is computer science.

F. M2: What do you do?
F2: Pardon?
M2: What do you do? I mean, what kind of job do you have?
F2: I'm a lawyer.

G. F1: I'm sure you've done a lot of traveling. What countries have you visited?
M1: I'm sorry. Could you please speak a little more slowly?
F1: Of course. I asked — what countries have you visited?
M1: I've been to several countries in Asia — Korea, Japan, Hong Kong, and Taiwan, but that's about all.

H. M2: How long have you been studying English?

F2: How long have I. . . ? I'm sorry. Would you mind repeating your question?

M2: Certainly. How long have you been studying English?

F2: Let's see. Ummm, for about two years.

UNIT 1, LISTENING PRACTICE, ACTIVITY 2: IDENTIFYING RELATIONSHIPS

A. F1: That was an excellent presentation, Ron.

M1: Thank you, Dr. Johnson. I worked hard on it all week.

B. M2: Great talk, Joan.

F2: Thanks, Frank. I hope I get a good grade, but you know how tough Mr. Thornton can be.

C. F1: Excuse me. I'm sorry to bother you, but would you happen to know what time it is?

M1: Certainly. It's five past two.

D. M2: Hey, what time is it?

F2: It's about two. Hurry up or we'll be late for class.

E. F1: Would you mind making five photocopies of this report, Don?

M1: Of course, Miss Lewis. I'll have them ready in five minutes.

F. M2: Cheryl, were you able to finish the report I asked you to type yesterday afternoon?

F2: Not yet. I still have the last section to do.

M2: O.K. Well, when do you think you can get it to me?

F2: Definitely by lunch time.

G. M1: We'd all really appreciate it if you could postpone the exam until next week. We have too much work to do this week.

F1: I'm afraid that won't be possible, Alan. You've all known about this exam for weeks.

H. F2: Bob, I think we need to talk about the report we just finished. Can we meet at 1:00 today?

M2: I usually go to lunch then, Carol, but. . . .

F2: Well, would 2:00 be okay?

M2: Sure. That'll be fine.

I. M1: So, how do you like it here?

F1: Oh, I'm really enjoying it. It's a nice change from being in school.

M1: I know what you mean. I felt the same way when I started working here.

F1: Well, I'm looking forward to getting to know everyone.

J. M2: My name is Edward Simpson.
F2: I'm sorry, but I'm afraid I didn't get your last name.
M2: It's Simpson.
F2: I'm pleased to meet you, Mr. Simpson.

UNIT 1, PRONUNCIATION PRACTICE, ACTIVITY 8: COUNTING SYLLABLES

One syllable	Three syllables
part	following
word	determines
group	expression
sound	correctly
think	consonant

Two syllables	Four syllables
number	dictionary
useful	repetition
pencil	understanding
pronounce	presentation
contain	experience

UNIT 1, PRONUNCIATION PRACTICE, ACTIVITY 9: COUNTING SYLLABLES

1. English
2. assignment
3. identify
4. course
5. neutral
6. important
7. similarities
8. nickname
9. official
10. raise
11. formality
12. review
13. stress
14. activities
15. count
16. communication

UNIT 1, PRONUNCIATION PRACTICE, ACTIVITY 10: FOCUSING ON WORD STRESS

1. CONduct   conDUCT
2. CONtrast   conTRAST
3. DEcrease   deCREASE
4. INcrease   inCREASE
5. INsult   inSULT

6.	OBject	obJECT
7.	PERmit	perMIT
8.	PRESent	preSENT
9.	PROGress	proGRESS
10.	PRODuce	proDUCE
11.	RECord	reCORD
12.	SUBject	subJECT

UNIT 1, PRONUNCIATION PRACTICE, ACTIVITY 11: IDENTIFYING STRESSED SYLLABLES

1.	preSENT	7.	PROGress
2.	reCORD	8.	inSULT
3.	CONtrast	9.	SUBject
4.	conDUCT	10.	PRODuce
5.	INcrease	11.	perMIT
6.	obJECT	12.	deCREASE

UNIT 1, PRONUNCIATION PRACTICE, ACTIVITY 12: IDENTIFYING STRESSED SYLLABLES

1.	attention	11.	opportunity
2.	example	12.	academic
3.	understand	13.	discussion
4.	difficult	14.	question
5.	introduce	15.	appropriate
6.	necessary	16.	pronunciation
7.	mistake	17.	audience
8.	relationship	18.	participate
9.	comprehension	19.	professional
10.	situation	20.	confident

B. UNIT 2

UNIT 2, LISTENING PRACTICE, ACTIVITY 1: IDENTIFYING EXPRESSIONS

A. F1: We had a terrible problem in the office this morning.
    M2: Oh, really? What happened?
B. M1: I saw a great movie last night.
    F2: You did? What was it?

C. F1: Mr. Kenrick fired three people yesterday.

M2: Three people? Who were they?

D. M2: I spent two hours last night doing my homework.

F1: Did you? Was it hard?

E. F2: I've been studying English for five years.

M1: I see. What level are you in now?

F. M2: My car broke down on the highway this morning.

F1: Oh, no! What did you do?

G. M1: I'm thinking of going to Paris for my vacation.

F2: Paris? That's great! When does your vacation start?

H. F1: I've been an accountant for five years now.

M2: Oh? What company do you work for?

UNIT 2, LISTENING PRACTICE, ACTIVITY 2: OPENING A CONVERSATION

A. M1: How do you like this weather?

F1: Well, it's too hot for me.

M1: Me too. And it's supposed to be even hotter tomorrow.

B. F2: Nice day, isn't it?

M2: Yes, it is. It's too bad we have to be inside all day.

F2: I know. I'd much rather be outside.

C. M1: Look at this line. It'll be a long wait.

F1: That's for sure. And I only have half an hour before my next class.

M1: You'll have to eat in a hurry to make it in time.

D. F2: Hi, John. How's it going today?

M2: Hi, Barbara. Oh, so-so. Actually, I've got a cold.

F2: Oh, I'm sorry to hear that. Are you taking anything for it?

E. M1: Hello, Denise. How are you?

F1: Oh, hi, Sam. I'm fine. How about you?

M1: Oh, I'm okay. What are you doing here?

F1: I need to return some books that are overdue.

F. F2: Excuse me. Do you know what time it is?

M2: Yes, it's about five to nine.

F2: Thanks. I guess we have a few minutes before the teacher gets here.

UNIT 2, LISTENING PRACTICE, ACTIVITY 3: CLOSING A CONVERSATION

A. M1: So, . . . it sounds like you had a great vacation.

F1: I did. I can't wait till the next one. . . . Anyway, . . . I see it's getting late. I'd better get going.

M1: You're right. It is getting late. I'll talk to you later.

F1: Okay. See you later. Good-bye.

M1: Good-bye.

B. F2: How did you like the movie?

M2: Frankly, I was a little disappointed. It had too much violence in it for my taste.

F2: I know what you mean. W-e-l-l, listen, I should be going. I still have a lot of work to do this afternoon.

M2: So do I. . . . Well, take it easy.

F2: You too. Bye.

C. M1: Thanks for helping me with this project, Ken.

M2: Oh, you're welcome. I'm glad I could be of some help.

M1: So-o-o-o, I'll let you get back to work now.

M2: Okay. Maybe we can get together for lunch one of these days.

M1: That sounds good. I'll give you a call later in the week. Thanks again. See you later.

M2: Okay. See you later.

D. F1: What happened at the meeting?

F2: Nothing. It was postponed until Monday.

F1: Oh, okay. It'll be interesting to see what happens. W-e-l-l, I know you're busy. I'll talk to you later.

F2: See you later.

F1: Good-bye.

UNIT 2, PRONUNCIATION PRACTICE, ACTIVITY 13: PRACTICING FINAL -ED SOUNDS

1.

need	needed
attend	attended
decide	decided
start	started
invite	invited
want	wanted
wait	waited
end	ended

	add	added
	visit	visited

2.	wash	washed
	like	liked
	talk	talked
	watch	watched
	walk	walked
	laugh	laughed
	help	helped
	stop	stopped
	work	worked
	finish	finished

3.	live	lived
	rain	rained
	play	played
	show	showed
	open	opened
	close	closed
	call	called
	enjoy	enjoyed
	rob	robbed
	use	used

UNIT 2, PRONUNCIATION PRACTICE, ACTIVITY 14: IDENTIFYING FINAL -ED SOUNDS

1.	miss	missed	I missed the bus yesterday.
2.	seem	seemed	You seemed very tired last week.
3.	practice	practiced	Jane practiced the piano for an hour.
4.	count	counted	The bank teller slowly counted the money.
5.	push	pushed	Many people pushed their way onto the bus.
6.	change	changed	The children changed their clothes in a hurry.
7.	learn	learned	Last year we learned how to give presentations in class.
8.	believe	believed	Nobody believed the truth.
9.	last	lasted	The movie lasted almost two hours.

10.	like	liked	When I was young, I liked to read comic books.
11.	hand	handed	The teacher handed out the tests in class.
12.	refuse	refused	Several students refused to do their homework.

UNIT 2, PRONUNCIATION PRACTICE, ACTIVITY 15: IDENTIFYING CORRECT PRONUNCIATION

1. Don <u>attended</u> class yesterday.
2. Laura <u>need</u> some help.
3. The meeting <u>end</u> at noon.
4. Class <u>started</u> on time.
5. Alice <u>want</u> to leave.
6. Jeff <u>decide</u> to move.
7. Louise <u>invited</u> me to the party.
8. My boss <u>waited</u> for an hour.
9. The teacher <u>hand</u> out the exams.
10. Pat <u>complete</u> the form.

UNIT 2, PRONUNCIATION PRACTICE, ACTIVITY 16: PRACTICING CORRECT PRONUNCIATION

1. Don <u>attended</u> class yesterday.
2. Laura <u>needed</u> some help.
3. The meeting <u>ended</u> at noon.
4. Class <u>started</u> on time.
5. Alice <u>wanted</u> to leave.
6. Jeff <u>decided</u> to move.
7. Louise <u>invited</u> me to the party.
8. My boss <u>waited</u> for an hour.
9. The teacher <u>handed</u> out the exams.
10. Pat <u>completed</u> the form.

C. UNIT 3

UNIT 3, LISTENING PRACTICE, ACTIVITY 1: LISTENING TO A STORY

Coming close to death can make a person feel more alive than ever before. Today I'd like to tell you about a close call with death I once had on one of the most dangerous roads in South America. Every time I think about it, I feel glad to be alive.

So, about two years ago, my friend and I were traveling on a crowded bus in the Andes mountains. The dirt road was very, very narrow — not even two lanes wide. A mountain wall went straight up on our right side. And on our left, the roadside dropped straight down thousands of feet into the thick Amazon jungle. Unfortunately, there was no fence to protect the cars and buses from going over the edge, although I'm not sure a fence would have been much help. Because we were traveling in the mountains, the road had many dangerous curves. Every time we came to a curve, the driver had to drive the bus out very close to the edge of the road so he had room to get around the curve without going over the edge. A lot of times it looked like he was going to drive straight off the road! My friend and I were sitting in the back of the bus, almost too afraid to look out the window.

When we were almost to the top of the mountain, the driver made a very wide turn. At exactly the same moment, another bus suddenly appeared, coming from the opposite direction. So there we were with another bus headed right at us! Both drivers immediately stepped on their brakes, but it was almost too late. The back left wheel of our bus went over the edge of the road and the bus began to lean over the side of the mountain. At that moment, I thought we were going to die. All the passengers started screaming, and that made me even more scared. After that, to make matters even worse, all the passengers moved over to the side of the bus to look out over the edge of the mountain. Of course, that made the bus start to lean even further. I thought the earth was moving under us! I guess a few other passengers thought so too, because they moved back to the other side of the bus. Then they jumped out of their windows onto the roadside. I think that's what saved us.

Meanwhile, the passengers from the other bus helped push our bus back onto the road as our driver slowly pulled forward. Finally, we all got back on the bus and continued safely down the mountain road into the Amazon jungle, very thankful to be alive. Two days later, my friend and I heard that an earthquake and heavy rain had destroyed that same mountain road several days after our trip. So, we came very close to death on that trip. Now, whenever I remember looking out that bus window over the mountain edge to the jungle far below, I feel very alive inside.

UNIT 3, LISTENING PRACTICE, ACTIVITY 2: IDENTIFYING EXPRESSIONS SHOWING TIME ORDER

A. So, about two years ago, my friend and I were traveling on a crowded bus in the Andes mountains.

B. Actually, after a while, we stopped looking out the window because it just made us more nervous.

C. When we were almost to the top of the mountain, the driver made a very wide turn.

D. At exactly the same moment, another bus suddenly appeared, coming from the opposite direction.

E. At that moment, I thought we were going to die.

F. After that, to make matters even worse, all the passengers moved over to the side of the bus to look out over the edge of the mountain.

G. Then they jumped out of their windows onto the roadside.

H. Meanwhile, the passengers from the other bus helped push our bus back onto the road as our driver slowly pulled forward.

I. Finally, we all got back on the bus and continued safely down the mountain road into the Amazon jungle, very thankful to be alive.

J. Two days later, my friend and I heard that an earthquake and heavy rain had destroyed that same mountain road several days after our trip.

UNIT 3, LISTENING PRACTICE, ACTIVITY 3: LISTENING TO A TALK

During this course, you will be participating in many small group activities. Today, I'd like to explain four main advantages of working in a small group to improve your speaking and listening skills in English.

The first main advantage of group work is that it gives students more language practice. In other words, students working in a group have more opportunities to practice speaking than in a class led by a teacher. Group work gives students a chance to use the skills, structures, and vocabulary that they are learning in class. This is important because people can't learn a language simply by studying rules or memorizing vocabulary lists. If students get more practice, then they can make faster progress in learning the language.

Another important advantage of group work is that many students feel more comfortable speaking in a group rather than in front of the entire class. For example, many students feel nervous when the teacher calls on them to speak in class. They worry about making a mistake in front of so many people. In a small group, however, students don't worry as much about making mistakes, so they participate more actively and more comfortably. If students feel more comfortable, then they participate more. As a result, they can learn more.

The third main advantage of group work is that it encourages students to share their ideas and knowledge. Group members learn to cooperate and to help each other. For example, if a student has trouble expressing an idea, that student can ask another group member for help instead of asking the teacher. This means that group members can take more responsibility for their own learning because they do not have to depend on the teacher for all their information. This is important because experts say that students learn more when they are actively involved in the learning process.

Finally, the fourth main advantage of group work is that it helps students develop important conversation skills. For instance, in a group discussion students practice taking turns, asking questions, agreeing, disagreeing, and so forth. This type of practice is important because it prepares students for using English in real-life situations.

In conclusion, then, I believe that group work has several important advantages. These are: one, more language practice; two, a more comfortable class atmosphere; three, more learner involvement; and finally, preparation for the real world.

UNIT 3, PRONUNCIATION PRACTICE, ACTIVITY 14: PRACTICING FINAL "S" SOUNDS

1.
watch	watches
teach	teaches
notice	notices
wash	washes
pronounce	pronounces
choose	chooses
judge	judges
miss	misses
speech	speeches
course	courses
box	boxes
class	classes
language	languages

	size	sizes
	bridge	bridges
	quiz	quizzes
2.	get	gets
	speak	speaks
	make	makes
	want	wants
	cost	costs
	book	books
	month	months
	sport	sports
	test	tests
	desk	desks
3.	wear	wears
	go	goes
	feel	feels
	answer	answers
	see	sees
	law	laws
	day	days
	problem	problems
	hobby	hobbies
	expression	expressions

UNIT 3, PRONUNCIATION PRACTICE, ACTIVITY 15: IDENTIFYING FINAL "S" SOUNDS

1.	belong	belongs	That book belongs to me.
2.	live	lives	Mary lives in New York.
3.	student	students	The students were early.
4.	close	closes	The store closes at six o'clock.
5.	tape	tapes	The tapes are in the language lab.
6.	drink	drinks	George always drinks coffee for breakfast.
7.	read	reads	Laura reads the newspaper every day.
8.	minute	minutes	I'll be ready to leave in ten minutes.
9.	finish	finishes	Rick usually finishes his homework before dinner.
10.	friend	friends	My friends are waiting for me.

11.	sentence	sentences	Please write those two sentences on the board.
12.	analyze	analyzes	That student always analyzes her mistakes.

UNIT 3, PRONUNCIATION PRACTICE, ACTIVITY 16 IDENTIFYING CORRECT PRONUNCIATION

1. The <u>bus</u> are late.
2. Mike often <u>miss</u> the bus.
3. The sun <u>rises</u> in the east.
4. Rita often <u>watches</u> TV.
5. Those new <u>dress</u> are expensive.
6. Two <u>class</u> were canceled yesterday.
7. Fran read ten <u>pages</u> last night.
8. Water <u>freeze</u> at 32 degrees Fahrenheit.
9. I speak several <u>languages</u>.
10. Dr. Smith <u>teach</u> class at 8:00.

UNIT 3, PRONUNCIATION PRACTICE, ACTIVITY 17: PRACTICING CORRECT PRONUNCIATION

1. The <u>buses</u> are late.
2. Mike often <u>misses</u> the bus.
3. The sun <u>rises</u> in the east.
4. Rita often <u>watches</u> TV.
5. Those new <u>dresses</u> are expensive.
6. Two <u>classes</u> were canceled yesterday.
7. Fran read ten <u>pages</u> last night.
8. Water <u>freezes</u> at 32 degrees Fahrenheit.
9. I speak several <u>languages</u>.
10. Dr. Smith <u>teaches</u> class at 8:00 every morning.

D. UNIT 4

UNIT 4, LISTENING PRACTICE, ACTIVITY 1: IDENTIFYING RIGHTS AND OBLIGATIONS

A. M1: I believe that people have a right to wear fur coats if they want to.

F1: I agree with you. In any case, protesters don't have a right to tell people what to wear.

B. F2: As I see it, people have a right to protest cruelty to animals. Animals can't protect themselves.

M2: Yes, that may be true, but, still, people have an obligation to follow the law.

C. M1: In my opinion, people have an obligation to protect animals. After all, wearing a fur is not a good reason to kill a living animal.

F1: I see what you mean, but I think people have a stronger obligation to respect other people's property.

D. F2: As far as I'm concerned, people don't have a right to ruin people's coats by throwing paint on them. It doesn't matter how strongly they feel about animal rights.

M2: I completely agree. Protestors have an obligation to respect other people's rights.

E. M1: As I see it, people don't have a right to kill animals for <u>any</u> reason.

F1: I'm afraid I can't agree with you. People all over the world kill animals for food, clothing, and many other things. I think the important point is that people have an obligation not to cause animals unnecessary pain.

UNIT 4, LISTENING PRACTICE, ACTIVITY 3: LISTENING TO A DISCUSSION

M1: In my opinion, reporters definitely should <u>not</u> carry out undercover investigations. I think it's an invasion of privacy.

F1: What do you mean?

M1: I mean that people have a right to know if someone is filming them. Everyone has a right to privacy. I feel that reporters shouldn't be making secret films of people.

F1: Yes, I agree that people have a right to privacy. However, in many of these cases, the reporters are investigating criminals. You know, they . . .

M1: Excuse me for interrupting, but are you saying that criminals don't have a right to privacy?

F1: No, that's not what I mean. But I believe that reporters have a right to videotape people when they're breaking the law. After all, the videotape is proof that someone is committing a crime, and . . .

M1: Sorry to interrupt, but . . . .

F1: Excuse me, but could I just finish this one point? Anyway, as I was saying, . . . with a videotape, a reporter has proof of what the person was doing. If people don't want to be videotaped breaking the law, then they shouldn't be breaking the law in the first place.

F2: May I say something here?

M1: Certainly.

F2: You know, reporters aren't police officers. They could be getting themselves into dangerous situations that they aren't able to control.

F1: Well, I don't think that happens very often. I mean, they aren't usually filming killers, or gangsters, or people like that.

M1: Well, I still don't think that reporters have a right to pretend to be someone they're not. In my opinion, that's lying. Reporters should be honest about who they are, even when they're getting a story.

F2: I see what you mean, but in these situations, the reporter is telling a small lie for a good reason. I mean, if the reporter can catch someone breaking the law, then that's more important than the "crime" of telling a lie.

M1: Yes, I completely agree with you.

F1: I'm afraid I don't agree at all. I guess we'll just have to agree to disagree on this subject.

UNIT 4, PRONUNCIATION PRACTICE, ACTIVITY 14: LISTENING TO SENTENCE STRESS

• **●** •

1. I'm finished.
   They're absent.
   I'm sorry.
   She's thinking.
   You told me.

● • **●**

2. Please begin.
   Take your time.
   Go to class.
   Joan was sick.
   Where's your book?

$\bullet \quad \bullet \quad \bullet \quad \bullet$

3. She sat at home.
   We helped the boss.
   They stopped to talk.
   He lived in Spain.
   They missed the bus.

$\bullet \quad \bullet \quad \bullet \quad \bullet \quad \bullet$

4. You asked a question.
   She watched the program.
   He needs to practice.
   She wrote a letter.
   The train was early.

$\bullet \quad \bullet \quad \bullet \quad \bullet$

5. He started to leave.
   We thought you were sick.
   She asked me to stay.
   I see what you mean.
   He opened the door.

$\bullet \quad \bullet \quad \bullet \quad \bullet \quad \bullet$

6. We've decided to leave.
   He explained it to Anne.
   We agreed to the plan.
   They discussed it with Frank.
   You can talk to your boss.

UNIT 4, PRONUNCIATION PRACTICE, ACTIVITY 15: IDENTIFYING SENTENCE STRESS

A. F1: Hello.
    M1: Hello. Is Bob there?
    F1: No, I'm afraid he's not here at the moment. Would you like to leave a message?
    M1: Yes. Could you ask him to call Tom Pearson?
    F1: Certainly. Does he have your number?
    M1: Yes, he does.
    F1: Okay. I'll give him the message as soon as he gets home.

M1: Thank you very much. Good-bye.
F1: Good-bye.

B. M2: Hello.
F2: Hello. May I speak to Susan?
M2: I'm afraid you have the wrong number.
F2: Oh? Isn't this 555-2654?
M2: No, it isn't. It's 555-2653.
F2: Oh, I'm sorry.
M2: That's okay. Good-bye.
F2: Good-bye.

C. F1: Hello.
M2: Hello. May I speak to Daniel?
F1: Yes, just a minute please.
M1: Hello. This is Daniel.
M2: Hi, Daniel. This is Ron.
M1: Oh, hi, Ron. How are you?
M2: Fine. Listen, am I catching you at a bad time?
M1: Actually, we were just sitting down to dinner. Could I call you back when we've finished?
M2: Of course. I'll talk to you later. Good-bye.
M1: Good-bye.

D. F2: [Recorded Message] Hello. I'm afraid I can't come to the phone right now. If you leave your name and phone number after the beep, I'll get back to you as soon as I can. [Beep]
M1: Hello. This is Jeff Walters calling. Kathleen, I need to ask you a question about work. Could you give me a call when you get home? Thanks.

UNIT 4, PRONUNCIATION PRACTICE, ACTIVITY 16: LISTENING FOR MISSING CONTENT WORDS IN A PASSAGE

Government officials feel that it is essential to start controlling population growth. The reason for this is that the government simply cannot take care of the growing number of people in the country. Poverty, unemployment, and a lack of housing are just some of the serious problems that people face. Therefore, officials feel that they must try to control the number of children that couples have. One action that the government has taken is to pass laws that discourage families from having more than one child. For example, parents can send one child to school for free, but then they must pay very high fees for any other children in their family. These laws have caused a lot of controversy in the country. Many citizens believe that people have a right to have as many children as they want without government control. Government officials, on the other hand, believe that the government has an obligation to work for the greater good of society.

E. UNIT 5

UNIT 5, LISTENING PRACTICE, ACTIVITY 1: LISTENING TO A PRESENTATION

As I was walking from the subway to work yesterday, at least four panhandlers asked me for money. In fact, the same thing happens every time I walk to work, and it's gotten so bad that I hate walking in the city. I feel that panhandlers have really taken control of the streets of this city. They're not only standing on sidewalks, but they're also in parks, in public buildings, and in bus stations. They stand in front of shops and they block entrances to the subway. In my opinion, panhandlers have become a serious social problem. Certainly, I think that poor and homeless people need our help. I feel very sorry for these people. However, I believe that giving money is not a good way to help. Today, then, I'd like to discuss three main reasons that I believe you should not give money to panhandlers.

In the first place, giving money to panhandlers does not solve their real problems. Many panhandlers suffer from serious problems such as mental illness, drug addiction, or alcoholism. They need to go to agencies that can provide long-term help for their problems. These agencies can give permanent help by providing job counseling or drug and alcohol rehabilitation. By giving panhandlers money, you discourage them from trying to get more permanent help. In fact, you may make their situation even worse because they use the money you give them to buy alcohol or drugs.

The second reason that you shouldn't give money to panhandlers is that you are helping make the city streets frightening and dangerous for pedestrians. In fact, giving money encourages panhandlers to continue begging. You make it possible for them to stay on the streets. The problem is that many of these panhandlers do not simply ask quietly or politely for a handout; a lot of them demand money from people. Some panhandlers scare people by shouting at them, following them, or blocking their way if they refuse to hand over money. Not all panhandlers are so aggressive, but many pedestrians are afraid to walk down the streets of their own cities, even during daylight hours. They simply don't know how to deal with so many panhandlers asking for money. Some people say that panhandlers have a right to stand in public places asking for money. However, I believe that city residents have a right to feel safe walking down the streets of their own city. Even if panhandlers in the street don't bother you, think of all the people they do disturb. By giving money, you keep the city streets dangerous for everyone else.

My third and final reason for not giving panhandlers money is that many of them are able to work, but they are lazy. They enjoy the freedom of not having to go to work every day. They don't want to work long hours for low pay, so begging is an easy way to get money without working. By giving them money, you just discourage them from looking for a real job. If they can get enough money from panhandling, why should they look for a job? Other panhandlers have signs saying that they are hungry or need to feed their families. However, when you give them money, they buy cigarettes, alcohol, or drugs instead of food. The problem is that you don't know which people will put your money to good use and which ones will not.

In conclusion, I definitely feel that panhandlers need our help. However, I think that giving them money is not a good way to help them. So, what should you do instead of giving money? One way you can help is to donate money to an organized charity that helps needy and homeless people. Another way you can help is to donate your time by volunteering to help in a homeless shelter. And a final way you can help is by writing to government officials to put pressure on them to provide more services and more help for homeless people.

Thank you. I'll be happy to answer any questions that you may have.

UNIT 5, PRONUNCIATION PRACTICE, ACTIVITY 15: LISTENING TO UNSTRESSED WORDS IN SENTENCES

1. Stressed form — a
    Unstressed form: They're in a hurry.
    I'll be there in a minute.
    That's not a problem.
    Mary's a teacher.

2. Stressed form — an
   Unstressed form: We'll leave in *an* hour.
   I have *an* idea.
   He's *an* engineer.
   It was *an* interesting discussion.

3. Stressed form — the
   Unstressed form: What's *the* problem?
   Room 204 is on *the* right.
   Their books are under *the* table.
   Stand in front of *the* class.

4. Stressed form — of
   Unstressed form: I talked to a lot *of* people.
   I'd like a copy *of* the report.
   She's one *of* the best managers here.
   I have a different point *of* view.

5. Stressed form — or
   Unstressed form: You can come by bus *or* subway.
   She spoke for five *or* six minutes.
   We walked three *or* four blocks.
   Take one *or* two deep breaths.

6. Stressed form — and
   Unstressed form: Bob *and* Jane were late.
   Speak clearly *and* slowly.
   Try to arrive between one *and* one-thirty.
   Keep your comments *and* questions brief.

7. Stressed form — for
   Unstressed form: I sat there *for* an hour.
   He did it *for* free.
   They're ready *for* the test.
   That's enough *for* now.

8. Stressed form — to
   Unstressed form: They have a right *to* privacy.
   She'd like *to* talk *to* you.
   I need *to* see the manager.
   We'll be there from three *to* four.

UNIT 5, PRONUNCIATION PRACTICE, ACTIVITY 16: LISTENING FOR DIFFERENCES

1. A. Pat's here.
   B. Pat isn't here.

2. A. Those people are paying attention.
   B. Those people **aren't** paying attention.
3. A. Mary was upset with her boss.
   B. Mary **wasn't** upset with her boss.
4. A. The speakers were well-organized.
   B. The speakers **weren't** well-organized.
5. A. Carol has studied French.
   B. Carol **hasn't** studied French.
6. A. The students have worked hard.
   B. The students **haven't** worked hard.
7. A. You can take a break now.
   B. You **can't** take a break now.
8. A. Ron should speak to his boss about that.
   B. Ron **shouldn't** speak to his boss about that.

UNIT 5, PRONUNCIATION PRACTICE, ACTIVITY 17: LISTENING TO STRESSED AND UNSTRESSED FORMS

1. A. M1: Can we leave now?
   B. F1: I'm not sure if we can.
   C. F2: We can leave in a few minutes.
2. A. F1: Is Tom absent?
   B. M2: I don't know if he is.
   C. M1: I think he's coming late.
3. A. F2: Were the students angry?
   B. M1: I think they were.
   C. F1: No, I think they were tired.
4. A. M2: Are the books expensive?
   B. F1: Yes, they are.
   C. M1: It seems to me they're reasonable.
5. A. F2: Have your friends left yet?
   B. M2: I believe they have.
   C. F1: Yes, they've left.

UNIT 5, PRONUNCIATION PRACTICE, ACTIVITY 18: IDENTIFYING AFFIRMATIVE AND NEGATIVE STATEMENTS

1. Robert isn't a student.
2. I think we should take the bus.
3. She can get a visa later.
4. Mary hasn't done her homework.
5. My boss wasn't happy with my report.

6. There were a lot of people at the party.
7. I can't speak Spanish.
8. I wasn't talking on the phone for very long.
9. The secretary has typed the letter.
10. You shouldn't take cash with you.
11. We're having a meeting this afternoon.
12. They weren't waiting in the classroom.

F. UNIT 6

UNIT 6, LISTENING PRACTICE, ACTIVITY 1A: CONSIDERING CONSEQUENCES

M1: What do you think about the interview?

F1: In my opinion, it's a terrible idea. I think it will give the killer just what he wanted in the first place — a lot of publicity. And everybody will be talking about him again.

M1: I know. He'll be happy that he's famous. That just doesn't seem right to me.

F1: I know what you mean.

M1: Yeah, the interview makes the murder seem like entertainment.

F1: Right. And the interview is also like a reward for his crime. I just don't think that's a message we should be sending.

M1: I agree. I'm worried that the interview might encourage other sick people to try the same thing. I mean, completely unknown people think they can become famous overnight by murdering someone.

F1: The interview will also give the author of the book a lot of publicity. Just think of all the money he'll be earning.

M1: I know. The interview will definitely increase his book sales.

F1: Yeah, that really bothers me.

M1: It bothers me too. It means that people are earning money — getting benefits — from a terrible murder.

F1: I also think that this kind of interview causes the family even more pain.

M1: Of course. I completely agree with you. A TV interview like this could really upset his family and friends. After all, they don't want to be reminded of the killing — even after so many years.

F1: You know, some people say that this kind of an interview might have some positive effects.

M1: Really? Like what?

F1: Well, they say the interview might help people understand what causes a person to commit such terrible crimes.

M1: Well, I don't know. I think the disadvantages outweigh the advantages. As far as I'm concerned, broadcasting the interview is a bad idea. I'm definitely not going to watch it on television.

F1: Me neither.

UNIT 6, LISTENING PRACTICE, ACTIVITY 1B: CONSIDERING CONSEQUENCES

A. M1: What do you think about the interview?

    F1: In my opinion, it's a terrible idea. I think it will give the killer just what he wanted in the first place — a lot of publicity. And everybody will be talking about him again.

B. M1: I know. He'll be happy that he's famous. That just doesn't seem right to me.

    F1: I know what you mean.

C. M1: Yeah, the interview makes the murder seem like entertainment.

D. F1: Right. And the interview is also like a reward for a crime. I don't think that's a message we should be sending.

E. M1: I agree. I'm worried that the interview might encourage other sick people to try the same thing. I mean, completely unknown people think they can become famous overnight by murdering someone.

F. F1: The interview will also give the author of the book a lot of publicity. Just think of all the money he'll be earning.

    M1: I know. The interview will definitely increase his book sales.

G. F1: Yes, that really bothers me.

    M1: It bothers me too. It means that people are earning money — getting benefits — from a terrible murder.

H. F1: I also think that this kind of interview causes the family even more pain.

    M1: Of course. I completely agree with you. A TV interview like this could really upset his family and friends. After all, they don't want to be reminded of the killing — even after so many years.

I. F1: You know, some people say that this kind of an interview might have some positive effects.

    M1: Really? Like what?

    F1: Well, they say that the interview might help people understand what causes a person to commit such terrible crimes.

J. **M1:** Well, I don't know. I think the disadvantages outweigh the advantages. As far as I'm concerned, broadcasting the interview is a bad idea. I'm definitely not going to watch it on television.

   F1: Me neither.

UNIT 6, LISTENING PRACTICE, ACTIVITY 2: GETTING CLARIFICATION

SEGMENT A

M2: In my opinion, doctors have an obligation to report pilots who use drugs to the authorities.

F2: I'm not sure what you mean.

M2: I mean that if a pilot goes to a doctor for treatment, then the doctor must report that pilot's name to airline officials.

SEGMENT B

F1: As far as I'm concerned, doctors have an obligation to keep this information confidential.

M1: Sorry, but I don't understand what you mean by confidential.

F1: Keeping information confidential means keeping it private or secret. . . . you know, not reporting it to anyone.

SEGMENT C

M2: Well, I understand the importance of patient confidentiality. However, it seems to me that doctors have a more important obligation to protect the public from possible harm.

F2: Let me see if I understand you. You believe that protecting patient confidentiality is more important than protecting the public good?

M2: No, actually I'm saying exactly the opposite. I think the most important consideration should always be protecting the public good.

SEGMENT D

F1: I think that doctors have an obligation to protect their patients' privacy. You know, if pilots trust doctors to keep their names secret, then more pilots will try to get medical help.

M1: So you mean that trust is essential in a doctor-patient relationship?

F1: Exactly.

74

SEGMENT E

M2: Well, as I see it, doctors have an obligation to take immediate action if they believe a patient is a threat to society. They can't worry about all the other pilots out there.

F2: Could you explain what you mean by "a threat to society?"

M2: Of course. In this case, I mean that a pilot is a threat or a danger to society because he risks hundreds of lives when he's flying an airplane.

SEGMENT F

F1: I think it's important to stop as many pilots as possible from using drugs. If doctors start reporting the names of pilots getting drug treatment, then other pilots will be afraid to get treatment. And that certainly won't protect the public.

M1: Are you saying that doctors will make the situation even worse if they report pilots to the authorities?

F1: Yes, that's exactly my point.

UNIT 6, PRONUNCIATION PRACTICE, ACTIVITY 14: LINKING WITH VOWELS

1. turn on   Please turn on the lights.

2. get off   Let's get off the bus.

3. take off   Please take off your coat.

4. put away   Put away your books.

5. look into   We have to look into the problem.

6. find out   It's time to find out the truth.

7. make up   You can't make up the test.

8. give up   Don't give up yet.

UNIT 6, PRONUNCIATION PRACTICE, ACTIVITY 15: LISTENING TO LINKING IN PAST TENSE VERBS

1. The students showed us the campus.

2. We lived in Los Angeles.

3. I called up my friend.

4. Several companies closed at noon.

5. They finished at six o'clock.

6. We turned up the radio.

UNIT 6, PRONUNCIATION PRACTICE, ACTIVITY 16: IDENTIFYING PAST TENSE VERBS

1. Those stores open at ten.
2. They walked into class late.
3. People laugh at the teacher's jokes.
4. We complained about poor service.
5. I talk about my boss.
6. We studied English grammar.
7. They stayed at the office.
8. I work until midnight.

UNIT 6, PRONUNCIATION PRACTICE, ACTIVITY 18: LINKING WITH CONSONANTS

1. next time — We'll do that next time.
2. bad day — We had a bad day.
3. some memos — He wrote some memos.
4. same mistake — They made the same mistake.
5. fair report — She wrote a fair report.
6. cheap pen — I bought a cheap pen.

UNIT 6, PRONUNCIATION PRACTICE, ACTIVITY 19: LISTENING TO LINKING

1. She can never come here again.
2. That's the first time you've said it.
3. I wish she'd leave.
4. Her friend died.
5. The manager wrote several letters.
6. We bought two computers.
7. Paul went to sleep early.
8. The teacher ran to class.

9. Please continue with this activity.

10. I'll let you get to work.

G. UNIT 7

UNIT 7, LISTENING PRACTICE, ACTIVITY 1: EVALUATING SEVERAL SOLUTIONS

A. SUGGESTED SOLUTION
M1: I think schools should offer classes to teach children how to handle anger.

    1. F1: Yes, I think that's a good idea, but do you think students can apply what they learn in these classes to real life? I mean, do you think these classes would really work?

    2. M2: I know what you mean, but are there enough teachers trained in the right techniques to teach these kinds of classes to students?

    3. F2: Do you think kids would agree to take these kinds of courses without being forced? The kids who need these classes the most would probably be the ones who wouldn't take them.

B. SUGGESTED SOLUTION
F1: In my opinion, the government needs to provide family counseling to families who need it.

    1. M1: The problem is that therapists say that this kind of counseling takes a long time to get results — from twelve to eighteen months, at least.

    2. F2: I think family counseling is really helpful, but I'm afraid it's much too expensive. The government simply can't afford it.

    3. M2: I think family counseling can be very successful because it gets the whole family working together. It doesn't isolate the teenager from the family.

C. SUGGESTED SOLUTION
M1: Personally, I believe that the government should spend more money on recreational facilities for teenagers. These kids need a place to go after school where they won't get into trouble.

    1. F2: I agree, but I'm afraid the government doesn't have enough money to build facilities for teenagers.

2. M2: I'm not sure I agree with that solution. In my opinion, teenagers need to spend time with their parents, not off somewhere playing basketball in a teen center. I don't think this solution really addresses the problem.

3. F1: Also, do we have trained people to supervise these facilities? It seems to me that this just isn't a workable idea.

D. SUGGESTED SOLUTION

F2: As far as I'm concerned, schools need to offer classes to parents to teach them effective parenting skills. You know, they can teach parents how to discipline their children, how to set limits, and so forth.

1. M1: I'm afraid most parents will never agree to attend classes like that unless they're forced to.

2. F1: Well, I'm not sure that parents have time to attend, or maybe they won't <u>make</u> time to attend classes like that.

3. M2: Who's going to pay for all these classes? After all, the city doesn't have enough money to pay for basic education of the students as it is.

4. M1: I don't know. Where are we going to get teachers to teach these classes? Who will organize these classes? I believe that this solution is much more complicated than you think.

UNIT 7, LISTENING PRACTICE, ACTIVITY 2: EVALUATING PARENTAL RESPONSIBILITY LAWS

SEGMENT A

M1: Well, one solution some people recommend is holding parents responsible for violent crimes their children commit. You know, if a teenager commits a crime, then the parents can also be charged with that crime.

F1: Is that possible? How do you hold parents responsible for their children's actions?

M1: Well, many states have already passed these kinds of laws. They're called parental responsibility laws.

F1: I don't know. I mean, will people go along with laws like that? After all, you can't expect parents to spend all their time following their kids around to make sure they don't commit any crimes.

SEGMENT B

M1: Yes, but if parents realize that they are legally responsible for their children's crimes, then they will <u>have</u> to take steps to get control of them.

F1: Ummm, . . . I see your point, but many teenagers live with a single parent. And in most cases, that parent has to have a job to support the family. How do you expect a parent who's in jail to support a family? I just don't think it's a very workable idea.

SEGMENT C

M1: Well, you may be right. Also, it may not be very practical or realistic to expect people on a jury to send parents to jail for their children's crimes. People on juries will probably feel sorry for the parents.

F1: Yes, and if people on the jury have children, they'll probably realize that parents can't always control their children, no matter how hard they try.

M1: I'll have to go along with you there.

SEGMENT D

F1: And don't forget that there may be other children living at home. Do you want to take money away from the family so the mother or father can pay a fine?

M1: Okay, I see your point. That might make the problem even worse. Most families don't have enough money as it is.

F1: Yes, I certainly don't think it will solve the problem.

SEGMENT E

M1: And besides, putting people in prison costs the state a lot of money. I think it would be better to spend that money on education or recreational facilities for teenagers rather than on punishing their parents.

F1: I agree with you.

SEGMENT F

M1: Well, parental responsibility laws might work in the long run. But I think it would take a long time for these laws to have any effect on the way that parents deal with their children.

F1: You might be right. Well, I think we agree that the disadvantages outweigh the advantages. What other possibilities are there?

79

UNIT 7, PRONUNCIATION PRACTICE, ACTIVITY 11:
LISTENING TO QUESTIONS WITH RISING INTONATION

1. Is that right?
2. Are we ready to begin?
3. Was that legal?
4. Do we all agree?
5. Does everybody understand the problem?
6. Did you summarize the situation?
7. Has everyone made a decision?
8. Have you all finished?
9. Will this improve the situation?
10. Can we afford this plan?
11. Should we try a different solution?
12. May I ask you a question?

UNIT 7, PRONUNCIATION PRACTICE, ACTIVITY 12:
LISTENING TO INTONATION

1. Ready?   Ready.
2. Now?   Now.
3. Okay?   Okay.
4. Right?   Right.
5. Wrong?   Wrong.
6. Yes?   Yes.
7. No?   No.
8. Definitely?   Definitely.
9. Really?   Really.
10. At work?   At work.

UNIT 7, PRONUNCIATION PRACTICE, ACTIVITY 13:
DISTINGUISHING QUESTIONS FROM STATEMENTS

1. Yesterday?
2. A meeting?
3. Seven o'clock.
4. A new computer?
5. Definitely.
6. For sure?
7. You think so?
8. Excellent.
9. That's great.
10. Excuse me?
11. Of course.
12. For instance?
13. Three people.
14. I see.
15. Really?
16. A quiz?

UNIT 7, PRONUNCIATION PRACTICE, ACTIVITY 14: LISTENING TO QUESTIONS WITH FALLING INTONATION

1. Who's your boss?
2. What's your opinion?
3. What do you mean?
4. What was the problem?
5. Which solution is the best?
6. Where did they hold the meeting?
7. When should we begin?
8. Why do you think that?
9. How do you spell that?
10. How long did the meeting last?
11. How much was the bill?
12. How many people have you met?

UNIT 7, PRONUNCIATION PRACTICE, ACTIVITY 15: IDENTIFYING RISING OR FALLING INTONATION

(R indicates rising intonation and F indicates falling intonation)

1. [R] Are we ready to get started?
2. [R] Have you studied this solution carefully?
3. [F] How much will this plan cost?
4. [R] Can we afford it?
5. [R] Is it worth the cost?
6. [F] How long will it take to get results?
7. [R] Will it have an immediate effect?
8. [F] How practical is this solution?
9. [F] What kind of changes will we have to make?
10. [F] What facilities do we need?
11. [F] How can we get the other resources that we need?
12. [F] How will people react to this plan
13. [R] Does this plan seem fair?
14. [R] Does the plan seem reasonable?
15. [R] Do you think this will solve the problem?
16. [F] How will this improve the situation?